THE NATIONAL ROAD

That a road should cross America from Atlantic to Pacific, as straight as possible, was a dream of Thomas Jefferson's. Before the West was mapped, before white men had crossed the Rockies, when few settlers had even ventured beyond the Alleghenies, Jefferson foresaw the need to bind the nation together from east to west by an artery of transport and communication. That route now exists, right across the nation's mid-section, and this book tells the three centuries of history behind it.

THE
NATIONAL ROAD

HOW AMERICA'S VISION OF A TRANSCONTINENTAL
HIGHWAY GREW THROUGH THREE CENTURIES
TO BECOME A REALITY

OLIVE W. BURT

*ILLUSTRATED WITH PHOTOGRAPHS AND
WITH MAPS BY ELLEN VIERECK*

THE JOHN DAY COMPANY
New York

Copyright © 1968 by Olive W. Burt

Library of Congress Catalogue Card Number: 68-11307

PRINTED IN THE UNITED STATES OF AMERICA

For Alice B. Nichols
who shares my love of history and
of old books

CONTENTS

THE NATIONAL ROAD

INTRODUCTION

A road, any road, is an interesting thing to study. It was built for some definite purpose — to help folks get together or to help them get away from each other. Along its route historical events have very likely taken place. A road is alive, not only with what is seen and heard as we travel over it, but with things that must be only felt or remembered or imagined. And of all the roads in this country, probably none has more historic interest than the great National Road, and the modern transcontinental highway that grew out of it.

The National Road itself was not very long compared with to-day's highways. It reached only from Cumberland, Maryland, to Vandalia, Illinois; from the Potomac to the Kaskaskia rivers, not quite six hundred miles. But its length was not the measure of its importance.

Before it was built, most travel in this newly settled country was in a north-south direction, along the rivers which served as highways. There were no roads by which one could travel from the eastern settlements into the western regions. There were Indian trails and buffalo tracks, but these were not of much use because they seldom went where the white man wanted to go.

The French had started the exploration and settlement of Canada before the British came to the New World. They floated down the Mississippi and established a few small outposts along its banks. It seemed as if this river, with the Ohio, might have to be the western boundary of the land that England could claim. The British were determined that this should not happen. Disputes with the French led to the French and Indian War, but the French still held the land west of the great river.

After the Revolution and the separation from England, the leaders of the new United States took up the problem. They were beginning to feel that their country could not be so limited. Some even dreamed of a time when the new nation would stretch from the Atlantic to the Pacific. They did not relish the idea of a foreign country's holding the land just across a river. In 1803 the United States purchased France's holdings along the Mississippi and westward — no one knew just how far.

Now it was more necessary than ever to have roads into the West. In March of 1806, Congress passed a bill providing for the construction of a road from Cumberland in northern Maryland to the Ohio country. For the first time, Federal money (money provided by the United States Treasury) would be used to make some improvement in the interior of the country. And this improvement would be a fine road.

When the Road became a reality, it was a great move toward uniting the country. It not only bound east and west together physically but gave the whole country an idea over which to become excited. And folks were excited. Everyone talked about the new venture. They gave it fond nicknames: the Cumberland; the Ohio

Road; Uncle Sam's Highway; the Great Western Turnpike; the United States Road; or, simply, the Road.

There were reasons why the National Road began and ended where it did. It started at Cumberland because at that time Cumberland was the end of the road westward out of Maryland. From Washington and Baltimore and cities farther south, roads came to this town and stopped. From there, westering travelers had to follow a hastily built path to the Monongahela River. Then they embarked on the long trip down this river to the Ohio, and down the Ohio to the interior. The new road would cut across the Allegheny Mountains, getting rid of the tiresome boat journey.

The Road stopped at Vandalia not because that was the last settlement, which it wasn't, but because of political troubles and lack of money.

The great idea behind the National Road was to have, some time, a highway running straight west from the Atlantic to the Pacific. So the original Road was merely the beginning of a great transcontinental highway. But it was the beginning. As such, it played an important part in the story of the United States. Its history is filled with drama and color.

In order to see how the National Road came to be and to understand its part in our history, we have to look back more than a hundred and fifty years before the Road was authorized. We have to look back past Cumberland, Maryland, to the early settlements on the Atlantic seaboard. And we shall continue long after the last stone was laid on the original Road, to describe how the idea behind it was finally carried out. Our story will cover three centuries, from 1651 to today.

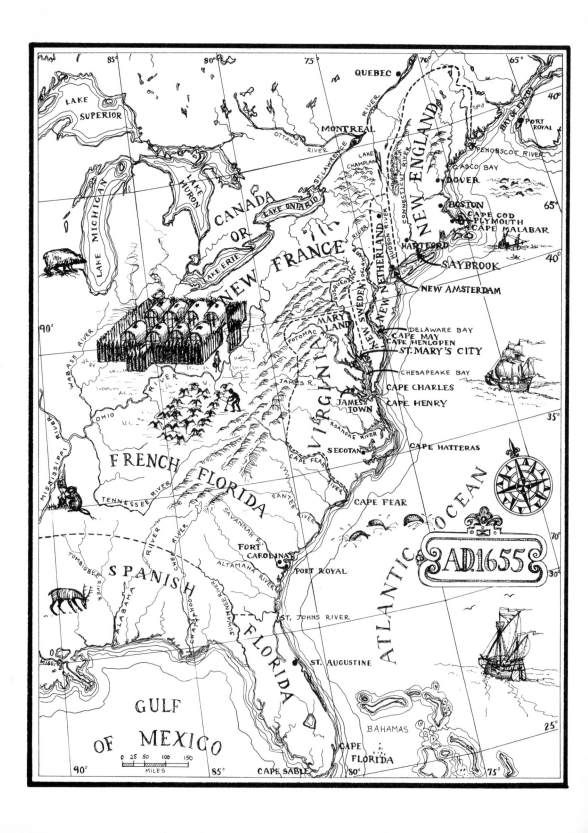

QUEBEC

LAKE SUPERIOR

LAKE MICHIGAN

LAKE HURON

LAKE ONTARIO

LAKE ERIE

OTTAWA RIVER

MONTREAL

ST. LAWRENCE RIVER

LAKE CHAMPLAIN

CANADA OR NEW FRANCE

BAY OF FUNDY

PORT ROYAL

PENOBSCOT RIVER

CASCO BAY

DOVER

NEW ENGLAND

BOSTON

CAPE COD
PLYMOUTH
CAPE MALABAR

CONNECTICUT RIVER

HARTFORD

SAYBROOK

NEW AMSTERDAM

HUDSON RIVER

NEW NETHERLAND

NEW SWEDEN (DELAWARE)

90°

WABASH RIVER

OHIO RIVER

DELAWARE BAY
CAPE MAY
CAPE HENLOPEN
ST. MARY'S CITY

MARY LAND

POTOMAC RIVER

SUSQUEHANNA RIVER

CHESAPEAKE BAY

CAPE CHARLES

VIRGINIA

JAMES R.

JAMES TOWN

CAPE HENRY

ROANOKE RIVER

SECOTAN

CAPE HATTERAS

FRENCH FLORIDA

MISSISSIPPI RIVER

TENNESSEE RIVER

CAPE FEAR RIVER

SANTEE R.

SAVANNAH R.

CAPE FEAR

ATLANTIC OCEAN

A.D. 1655

SPANISH

TOMBIGBEE RIVER

ALABAMA RIVER

CHATTAHOOCHEE RIVER

ALTAMAHA RIVER

FORT CAROLINA

PORT ROYAL

FLORIDA

SUWANNEE RIVER

ST. JOHNS RIVER

ST. AUGUSTINE

MISS. R.

GULF

OF MEXICO

0 25 50 100 150
MILES

BAHAMAS

CAPE FLORIDA

90°

85°

CAPE SABLE

80°

75°

1

THE STREET THAT LEADS TO YE WOODS

There was great excitement in New Sweden that June day of 1651. Tall, strong, coarsely dressed men poured from the small log houses at Fort Christina on the Delaware River. Women left off their household chores, their heads raised to listen. Then they hurried to join the men. Children in wooden shoes and homespun aprons clutched at their mothers' skirts, thumb-in-mouth as they watched, wide-eyed.

The cause of the stir was easily seen and heard. It was a small flotilla of eleven Dutch ships, coming down river with drums beating, horns blowing and flags flying. Dutch flags, these were, and the Swedes frowned at the sight of the foreign banners.

Along the decks of the wooden vessels strode armed and uniformed soldiers. Among these was a figure easily recognized by the watching Swedes. It was Peter Stuyvesant, Governor of New Nether-

An old Swedish log house, which once stood near the present junction of U.S. 40 and U.S. 13 outside New Castle, has been moved to the Delaware State Museum in Dover, where it may now be seen.

land to the north. He was staring with angry eyes at the rich meadowlands through which the Delaware made its way. The Swedes knew that the Dutch had come to take the land they claimed for Holland.

In 1609 Henry Hudson, sailing for the Dutch East India Company, had discovered the river that bears his name. He claimed the adjacent territory for Holland. The claim extended west to the Dela-

16

ware River, which rises in the Catskill Mountains in what is now New York State and flows southeastward to Delaware Bay. Between the two streams lies a lush land, at that time heavily forested and rich in rivers and lakes that teemed with the much-wanted beaver. The Dutch had established a few posts here and there to trade with the Indians. One such settlement had been started here on the Delaware, near where the Swedish fort now stood. But there had been trouble, and the angry Indians had demolished every vestige of the Dutch.

When two Swedish vessels arrived in the spring of 1638, the newcomers saw no sign that the land was claimed by others. They disembarked and chose a site for a fort on the west bank of the river, where Wilmington, Delaware, now stands. With Peter Minuit as commander, the Swedes claimed the land for their Queen Christina, and to make it legal, Minuit invited the Indian sachems to his cabin. From them he purchased "as much of the land in all parts and places of the river, on both sides" as he desired. He paid for the land with merchandise brought from his native country. The Indians sealed the pact by presenting beaver skins to the captain. Minuit immediately set about constructing his fort, which was named Fort Christina.

Now trouble began. Some thirty miles up the river, on the eastern bank, was the Dutch Fort Nassau, established twenty-five years earlier. When the Dutch discovered what was happening, they sent messengers down the river to protest. Now, after thirteen years of bickering, Peter Stuyvesant was taking stern measures.

It was not his first attempt to take this land by force. Some six weeks before this June morning, he had sailed down from Fort Nassau with one vessel. He had thought this would be enough, but he was wrong.

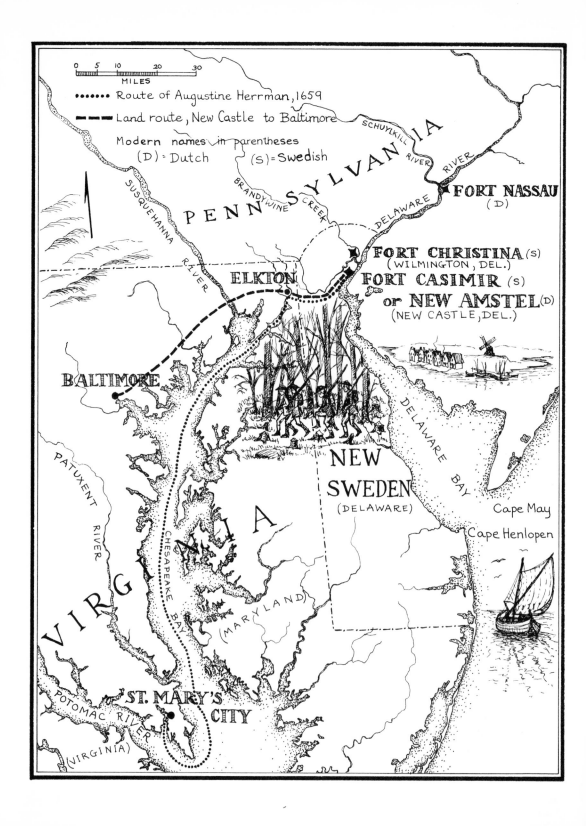

MILES
0 5 10   20   30

•••••• Route of Augustine Herrman, 1659

– – – Land route, New Castle to Baltimore

Modern names in parentheses
(D) = Dutch   (S) = Swedish

PENNSYLVANIA

SCHUYLKILL RIVER

RIVER

BRANDYWINE CREEK

DELAWARE

SUSQUEHANNA RIVER

FORT NASSAU
(D)

FORT CHRISTINA (S)
(WILMINGTON, DEL.)

ELKTON

FORT CASIMIR (S)
or NEW AMSTEL (D)
(NEW CASTLE, DEL.)

BALTIMORE

DELAWARE BAY

NEW
SWEDEN
(DELAWARE)

Cape May

Cape Henlopen

PATUXENT RIVER

CHESAPEAKE BAY

VIRGINIA

(MARYLAND)

POTOMAC RIVER

ST. MARY'S
CITY

(VIRGINIA)

Johan Printz, the governor of New Sweden, had not hesitated. He had called his fighting men together, boarded his own little barge, and with cannon and ammunition had set out to repel the invader.

Stuyvesant had placed his boat some three miles below Fort Christina. He slanted the boat across the channel, blocking the way. He, too, had guns. But when he saw the oncoming Swedish barge and noted the grim look on Governor Printz's face, the Dutchman thought better of his plan. Instead of trying to fight it out, he had quietly withdrawn.

Now he was back again, this time with a small armada. They sailed grandly down the river, making all the noise of a triumphant invading army.

This time Governor Printz saw that opposition was useless. There were not enough fighting men in all New Sweden to make a stand against this threat. Helplessly he watched the flotilla sweep down the river. Around him men, women and children stared and muttered in angry dismay.

On the deck of his own vessel, Peter Stuyvesant spoke to his aide. "This has been easy. Not a shot fired. Now keep a sharp lookout for a site for the fort we shall build. We want a place where the river narrows somewhat, so our guns can command the whole width of the stream. We'll have these Swedes penned in and can make them pay toll as they pass up and down the river. And not only the Swedes, but the British or anyone else who wishes to travel along this waterway. We'll collect toll on everything that moves up or down past our fort."

The aide nodded, but it was Stuyvesant himself who spied the sand spit stretching out into the river from the western bank. It was

Johan Printz, governor of New Sweden at the time the Dutch Fort Casimir was built.

exactly what he wanted. He ordered his vessels to put in to shore. Disembarking, he examined the site more closely.

The sand spit was firmly joined to the grassy verge of the river. Beyond it was a narrow strip of meadowland surrounded by the towering trees of the dark forest. The woods were gloomy and fearsome, the home of Indians and wild animals. No one ventured into the shadowy depths if he could help it.

But logs were needed for the fort, and Stuyvesant ordered his men into the forest to fell trees and drag them down to the sand spit. They went in small crews, with armed guards to protect them. The sound of their axes rang through the clear, bright air. The lovely trees, the hemlock, oak and elm, which had never before felt the bite of an ax, came crashing to the ground. Branches were lopped off and the naked trunks dragged down to the riverbank. There they were

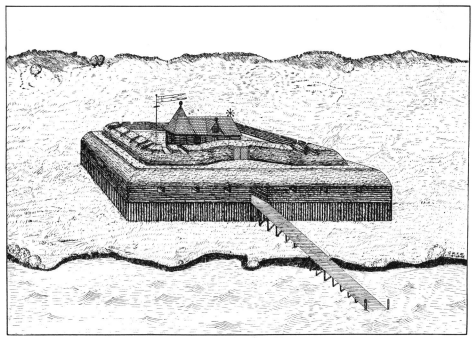

FORT CASIMIR.

hacked into shape, and laid, one above the other, to form the palisades and cabins of the Dutch fort, Casimir.

In the beginning, the road west was only this — the path to the forest and back that Stuyvesant's men had beaten to obtain the logs for Fort Casimir. Later, when a settlement grew up around the fort, the path was broadened into a street. The people gave it the name of "the street that leads to ye woods."

Peter Stuyvesant set to work to secure his hold on this rich land. He promised the natives all sorts of benefits and finally persuaded Chief Pemminack to sign over to the Dutch all the territory owned by his tribe. The chief was so flattered by the captain that he asked for nothing in return save that his gun should be kept in repair without cost and that whenever he came into the settlement and was hungry, he should be fed.

Governor Printz appealed to Sweden for assistance in taking back the land he claimed. But for a long time no help came, and the Swedes groaned under the tolls and taxes imposed on them. Not even a canoe could get past Fort Casimir without paying.

The Swedes, and the Poles and Finns who had come across the Atlantic with them, were of a fierce and independent nature. They could not endure being subservient to the Dutch. In earlier times, anyone could climb into a canoe and float down the river if he wished to get away. Now this was impossible. The only escape was by land, through the dangerous forest. With luck, a fugitive could reach the British settlements farther west and south, in Maryland or Virginia.

One by one, desperate men followed the street to the woods and then pushed onward. Sometimes they followed an Indian trail for awhile, or a bear or buffalo track. More often they had to make their own path, hewing it through the tangled maze of wild vines and undergrowth. Some took wife and children along; others went alone or with a companion or two. Some went a few miles into the forest and stopped beside a small stream, built a cabin and stayed on, living on game and wild berries. Others went ahead with grim determination till they reached a British settlement. These generally found a safe stream flowing southward. Then they built a canoe and ended their journey in the old way, by water.

Besides fugitives from the Dutch, there were traders who ventured through the forest to carry goods to the Indian villages to exchange for valuable furs. These, too, often made their own paths through the woods, and sometimes chose to stay with the natives.

In the years following the construction of Fort Casimir, the stronghold and the surrounding land passed from the Dutch to the Swedish and back again. By 1656 the settlement was called New Amstel. Hard times hit the village. Crops were poor, there was much sickness and the Dutch rulers were hard on the people. More and more escaped along the woodland trails leading south and west. But few, if any, records were kept of these journeys.

Then, some eight years after the Dutch had taken over, the governor of New Netherland sent an ambassador to the governor of Maryland at St. Mary's City. This settlement on the peninsula that formed the northern shore at the mouth of the Potomac River was then the capital of Maryland. It has now been restored as an historic site.

The ambassador's name was Augustine Herrman and he kept a careful record of his journey. From it we learn that there was at that time a fairly well established route between the Dutch and Swedish settlements and the British colonies to the south. Herrman and a companion, with some armed guards, were guided by Indians who knew the best trails. From New Amstel they went through the forest to the Elk River where it empties into Chesapeake Bay. There they took a canoe down the bay to their destination.

Later, this foot trail became a horse path, as communication between the settlements developed. Still later it was widened so that carts, then wagons, could pass over it.

In 1664 the British seized Fort Casimir and New Amstel from the Dutch. They destroyed the Dutch fort and changed the settlement's name to New Castle, the name the city bears today. With the British in control of this region, communication and travel between the various villages increased. The narrow forest trails were widened for carts and wagons. By 1750 there was a well-traveled route from New Castle to Baltimore. Some of the way, it is true, was generally by water — down the Elk River and Chesapeake Bay. The overland part was very poor. Stumps, underbrush, rocks and ruts endangered axles and horses. But in spite of these difficulties, it was used.

This section of road played an important part in our nation's history. For a time it was the post road, over which was carried the mail and the news from Massachusetts, New York and Pennsylvania to the colonies in the south. Benjamin Franklin rode along it and described its shortcomings in *Poor Richard's Almanac* for 1733. News of the Battle of Lexington was brought, posthaste, down this road. The delegates from the southern colonies to the Continental Congress in Philadelphia probably slogged their difficult way along it. In 1777 General Howe landed his British troops at the Head of Elk (now Elkton) at the top of Chesapeake Bay. He marched them along part of the old road in heading toward Philadelphia, where he hoped to catch General Washington's troops by surprise. General Lafayette's men marched southward over this route, and Washington's soldiers traveled it on their way to meet General Cornwallis at Yorktown and there defeat the British and win the Revolution.

In time the primitive road would know the creak of stagecoach wheels. Later still, the rails of one of the first railroads were laid along the old trail. No steam engine puffed at the head of this early train; the cars were drawn by horses, who undoubtedly found the wooden rails easier to negotiate than was the old, stump-infested path.

Today a paved highway, U.S. 40, follows closely the route of this old road. Southwest from New Castle, Delaware, to Elkton, Maryland, it traces the route of the old forest trail. From Elkton it swerves more sharply southwest, along the western shore of Chesapeake Bay to Baltimore.

2

PACK HORSE TRAILS

Major George Washington, just twenty-one years old, rode north from Williamsburg, Virginia, on the last day of October, 1753. He was dressed in fine broadcloth, as befitted a gentleman and an officer. But his pack horse carried a greatcoat, blankets and scarves to protect him against the cold he knew he would soon meet. He was on his way to the French outposts, somewhere far to the northwest beyond the Allegheny Mountains.

With the major, also suitably prepared for winter as he thought, rode Jacob van Braam, a Dutch fencing master. He knew French and was to act as interpreter. Two young Negro servants accompanied their master.

The little party traveled north and west to the busy town of Alexandria on the Potomac River. Then on they went, over the Blue Ridge Mountains and across the beautiful Shenandoah River to

Winchester, Virginia. This was the last place it would be possible to buy horses and supplies. Then on they went, always north and west, to the Ohio Company's post on Will's Creek in northwestern Maryland. Part of this route would be over a recently marked trail.

Four years earlier, Governor Robert Dinwiddie of Virginia had received word that King George II had granted the Ohio Company a vast tract of land along the Ohio River. The governor and other prominent Virginians were the officers of the Ohio Company. Conditions of the grant were that the company immediately choose its land and put settlers upon it.

In order to meet these terms, Governor Dinwiddie had sent out Thomas Cresap, with the Indian guide Nemacolin, to mark a trail to the point where Will's Creek entered the Potomac, near the Maryland-Pennsylvania border, and beyond to the Monongahela, if they could make it that far. Cresap was also to establish a post, or store, at the Will's Creek site.

The section of the route blazed by this party was named Nemacolin's Wilderness Path. It was wide enough only for horses, but it would serve well for the pack trains taking goods to the post and bringing furs down to Williamsburg.

When Cresap returned from his job, he reported that the French were pushing down into Virginia territory. They were setting up outposts along the Ohio and the Mississippi and were driving British traders and any Indians friendly to them out of these areas.

The officers of the Ohio Company felt sure that to get rid of the French would certainly mean war. But the canny Scottish governor felt it would be more economical in time, effort, money and men to persuade the French to leave.

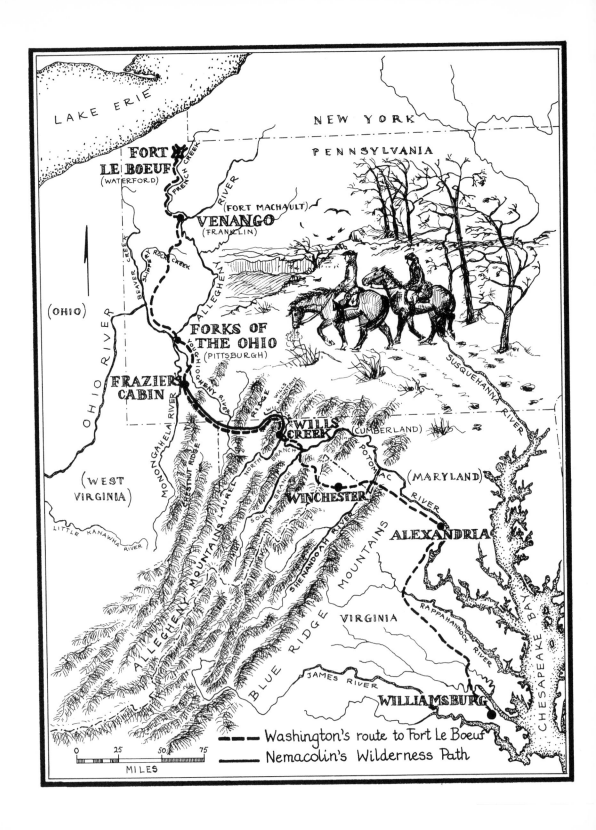

LAKE ERIE

NEW YORK

PENNSYLVANIA

FORT
LE BOEUF
(WATERFORD)

FRENCH CREEK

RIVER

(FORT MACHAULT)

VENANGO
(FRANKLIN)

SLIPPERY ROCK CREEK

BEAVER CREEK

ALLEGHENY

(OHIO)

OHIO RIVER

FORKS OF
THE OHIO
(PITTSBURGH)

YOUGHIOGHENY RIVER

FRAZIER
CABIN

MONONGAHELA RIVER

CHESTNUT RIDGE

LAUREL RIDGE

WILLS MOUNTAIN

WILL'S
CREEK

RIDGE

WILLS CREEK

(CUMBERLAND)

SUSQUEHANNA RIVER

(WEST
VIRGINIA)

LITTLE KANAWHA RIVER

NORTH BRANCH

POTOMAC

(MARYLAND)

WINCHESTER

SOUTH BRANCH

RIVER

ALEXANDRIA

ALLEGHENY MOUNTAINS

SHENANDOAH RIVER

BLUE RIDGE MOUNTAINS

VIRGINIA

RAPPAHANNOCK RIVER

CHESAPEAKE BAY

JAMES RIVER

WILLIAMSBURG

0   25   50   75
MILES

- - - Washington's route to Fort Le Boeuf
——— Nemacolin's Wilderness Path

"We'll try diplomacy first," he declared. "Let me have a tactful emissary to go to them and ask them to withdraw. If that fails, we can try sterner methods."

Governor Dinwiddie sent out a call for volunteers to do the job. Only one responded, the young George Washington. He had already spent four years working out-of-doors as a surveyor. His long, lean frame was tough; his disposition calm and steady. So here he was, at the beginning of winter, leading his small party into almost unknown regions.

It took fifteen days to reach the Ohio Company's post at Will's Creek. There Washington found Christopher Gist, another frontiersman employed by the company, waiting for him. There were also two traders to the Indians, Barnaby Currin and John McQuire. With these additions to his party, Washington was ready to go on. He wanted to keep the expedition as small as possible, so that it might move more swiftly and secretly through the forest and the mountains.

On November 15 the little band set out, bundled against the cold and wet of winter. For eight bitter, weary days they slogged along through mud and snow, always heading northwest toward the French fort which stood just a few miles south of Lake Erie. They followed Nemacolin's Wilderness Path for awhile, but before long they were forced to travel unmarked trails.

Through sleety rain and heavy snow, through cold and wet, the grim party wound its way up and down the slopes of the Alleghenies, through dense woodlands, across the Youghiogheny River, through swamps and over icy creeks to the Monongahela. On the evening of the eighth day they stopped at the cabin of James Frazier, a British trader to the Indians. They had averaged only fourteen miles a day.

Frazier had a good deal to tell the young officer. Early that spring, French soldiers had come to the Indian village of Venango, some seventy miles farther north, and had driven out the British traders who were living there.

"Some were taken prisoner," Frazier related angrily, "but I managed to escape. I came down here, thinking to be safe from those French bandits. And do you know? They destroyed both the Indian and the British dwellings and set to work to build a fort there — a French fort, mind you — which they are calling Fort Machault. Have no doubt, sir, the French intend to take and hold this land."

Young Washington listened to the older man. He saw in the fierce eyes peering from the bearded face a deep resentment of the treatment he had received. The major knew that this man would be a loyal aide if trouble developed.

"They make no secret of their intentions," the trader went on. "They boast about a fellow named La Salle. They say he explored all this region more than eighty years ago. They say he called the Ohio *La Belle Rivière* — the Beautiful River — and took the land on both sides in the name of the King of France!"

Major Washington nodded. He knew of these claims. He knew that the French kings had encouraged adventurers and Jesuit priests to explore widely in the New World and to convert the Indians to Christianity and the Catholic Church.

"Not content with these claims," Frazier continued, "just four years ago the governor of what they called New France sent a military expedition down the Ohio to convince the Indians that the land belongs to France. I was on the Ohio at that time. I saw what they did."

Interested, Washington leaned forward. His lean, six-foot-three body was all attention. His pockmarked face with its high cheek-bones, aristocratic nose and thin-lipped mouth was flushed by the heat from the fireplace. The flames glinted on his rust-colored hair, from which the carefully powdered wig had been removed.

"Tell me about it!"

"It was a great show! The leader was a fellow named Bien-ville —"

"Pierre Joseph Celaron de Bienville," Washington murmured. "Yes, I've heard of him."

"They came, this de Bienville and his soldiers, all dressed up in magnificent uniforms, with badges and ribbons and gold braid enough to bridge the Monongahela. And trumpets and drums! Flags waving! With great fanfare they nailed sheets of white iron to the trees, declaring these proved the region belonged to France. Nearby, along the shore, they buried lead plates with the same claim on them. The Indians were greatly impressed."

"But of course the land is England's!" Washington said firmly. "We purchased it from the Iroquois — paid for it — and have deeds from the Indians. The French must acknowledge our right!"

"They never will," the trader said gloomily. "They've ordered all British traders out of the region. It was after this that I went up to Venango, only to be driven away from there!"

"I carry dispatches to the French commander, ordering him to withdraw," the major explained. "Things must change here."

The next morning Washington sent his goods in canoes down the river. He, with Gist, van Braam and their servants, went by land. They followed the Monongahela toward the point where it joined

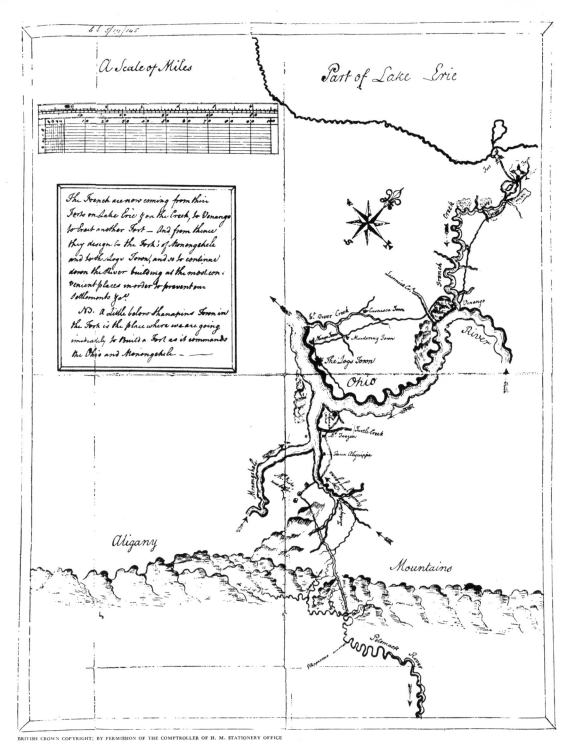

A reproduction of Major George Washington's own map. His comments on the journey may be more easily read on the copy opposite.

PART OF LAKE ERIE

FORT LE BOEUF

0 10 20 30 40 50 60 70 80 90 100
MILES

N

(Washington's map has been turned on this page so that North is straight up)

W ✦ E

S

FRENCH CREEK

VENANGO

RIVER

ALLEGHENY (called "OHIO" by Washington)

KUSKUSKI

BEAVER CR.

MURDERING TOWN

MINGO TOWN   THE LOGS TOWN

OHIO RIVER

TURTLE CREEK

SHANAPINS TOWN AT THE
FORKS OF THE OHIO
(called Forks of the
Monongahela by
Washington)

FRAZIER'S CABIN

YOUGHIOGHENY R.

GISTS PLACE

MONONGAHELA RIVER

MOUNTAINS

WILLS CREEK

POTOMAC RIVER

The French are now coming from
their Forts on Lake Erie (along)
the Creek, to Venango to erect
another Fort — And from thence
they design (plan) to the Forks of
Monongahela and to the Logs Town,
and so to continue down the River
building at the most convenient
places in order to prevent our
settlements (thereon).

NB. A little below Shanapins Town
in the Fork is the place where we
are going immediately to build a
Fort as it commands the Ohio
and Monongahela —
   (This Fort was named Fort Duquesne, later renamed Fort
Pitt, and now Pittsburgh)

LATER SITE OF FORT
CUMBERLAND

ALLEGHENY

- - - - - - - Washington's Route

the Allegheny to form the mighty Ohio. A wintry sun was setting when Washington stood and studied the site. The red glow from the sky cast an eerie light over the dark, bare trees, the icy rivers. It was a gloomy moment, but the young officer could see what this spot promised. He pointed it out to Gist.

"On that point of land a fort could be erected with little expense or trouble. It would command both rivers and the Ohio. Trade and travel could come to the very gate. I shall recommend that a post be built here."

That night there was a disturbance in camp. Washington stepped outside his tent to see what caused the trouble. He found four half-starved, half-frozen French traders begging for shelter. Gist wanted to drive them away. Let them starve or freeze! They were only Frenchies, and their countrymen had taken many a British trader's home. But Washington brought them inside, dried them out and gave them food. Then he questioned them.

They were deserters from the French Army, which had forced them into service. They had been down the Mississippi, building outposts. With van Braam interpreting, Washington learned much.

"Many Indians are on our side," one deserter boasted, "even though some are hostile. Last January we raided an Indian village where some British traders had taken shelter. One of these and a Miami chieftain were killed in the fray. Some of the traders were taken to Montreal as prisoners. Those Indians had to be taught that they can't help the British!"

"Governor Dinwiddie doesn't want war," Washington confided to Gist. "But it seems inevitable. However, I'll go on and deliver my message."

A few days later, Washington held a pow-wow with Half King, the leader of a federation of Delaware, Shawnee and Miami Indians. The chief was angry over the killing of his people by the French. He promised to help Washington. He persuaded two or three of his warriors to join him in leading the major's party to the French at the new Fort Machault.

This fort was under the command of Captain Joncaire, who received the young officer with courtesy, but with no indication that the French would pay any attention to the British demands. So Washington went on through the bitter weather to Fort Le Boeuf, fifteen miles south of the French outpost on the shore of Lake Erie. There he met the French Commander of the West, Gardeur de St. Pierre. This officer was an old, experienced trooper. He had lost an eye in battle some years before, but could still terrify the timid with the fierceness of his one good eye.

He must have been amazed at the youth and the cool authority of the soldier who had come so far through dangerous country in midwinter. But he received the major courteously, though his answer to the dispatch demanding his withdrawal was stern.

"I am here by order of my general, and I do not feel obliged to obey your governor's demand that I depart!"

Washington could get no more from him, and with the curt reply stowed away in his waterproof pouch, the major set out for Virginia and sunshine. By this time the young officer who had left Williamsburg so stylishly dressed nearly two months before, was clad in buckskins, stained and shrunken. An Indian "matchcoat" had replaced his broadcloth greatcoat. And he was afoot. His horse had grown so weak from cold and hunger that he could not carry a rider.

THE NATIONAL ROAD

In order to make better time himself, Washington put van Braam in charge of the horses, to lead them back over the trails. Washington and Gist set out cross-country toward the post on Will's Creek.

It was a terrible journey for the young officer who had been used to the comforts of a rich plantation. The two lonely travelers had to battle deep snow and bitter cold. They must break ice to get drinking water. They slept in wet clothes, without shelter. At one place they met two Indians, who professed to be friendly. Then, at the first chance, one took a shot at the Virginians. He was caught, and again Gist wanted to make short work of the traitor, but Washington let him go.

It was near the end of December when they came to the Allegheny River. It was frozen only partway across. The middle of the stream boiled along, hurtling dangerous chunks of ice and uprooted trees. The two companions spent a whole day making a raft on which to cross the river.

They managed to reach midstream, but there the current was so swift and the ice and debris so hazardous that it was difficult to manage the little raft. Washington tried to guide it with a pole, but a swirling log knocked this from his hand, jerking him into the icy water. He managed to grasp the edge of the raft and was pulled aboard. They made their way to a nearby island where, wet and miserable, they spent a dreadful night.

The next morning the stream was frozen over and the two men crossed on the ice. They struggled on to John Frazier's cabin, where they were grateful for warmth and food and shelter.

January was just two days old when the emissaries reached the

Ohio Company's post on Will's Creek. There Gist remained, but Washington obtained fresh horses and hurried on to report to Governor Dinwiddie.

Major George Washington's expedition had taken ten weeks of desperately difficult travel over little-known trails in midwinter. Though some of the time he was afoot, the paths were generally wide enough for horses. Much of this was due to the work of Thomas Cresap and Chief Nemacolin. They had marked trails over which British traders could take animals loaded with goods to trade to the Indians.

Some of Washington's route would later become a part of the National Road, particularly the section known as Nemacolin's Wilderness Path. Probably more important to the National Road, however, was Washington's grim decision that a road to the West must be built if British subjects were to be protected from French encroachments.

Washington made this recommendation to Governor Dinwiddie, and throughout the remainder of his life he held firmly to this idea.

As for the young officer's reward for doing a job no one else would undertake, for his suffering in the service of the king, he wrote, "I was employed to go on a journey in the winter (when I believe few or none would have undertaken it) and what did I get by it? My expenses borne!"

3

THE TRAMP OF SOLDIERS

Governor Dinwiddie listened to Major Washington's report. The older man's plump and rosy face was grim.

"Then it must be war, you think? The French won't give up without a fight?"

"But if there is war," the officer pointed out, "we must have a road, sir. A road over which heavy artillery wagons can travel — not just a pack horse trail."

"We can lay down a road. That is no problem."

Washington's thin lips curved in a wry smile. "You think not, sir? You haven't seen that land. The forests are very dense — miles of giant oak and walnut, tough enough to shatter an ax blade, and all twisted and tangled with vines and undergrowth. Streams overflow their banks; the lowlands are impossibly boggy; the slopes too steep for any wagon. Building a road there will take time, effort and hundreds of laborers."

"There will be time for that," the governor insisted. "I have sent Captain William Trent out with a company of men to build a fort at the fork of the Ohio — where you recommended one should be erected. I've learned that the French would like to take over that site. I told Trent to beat them to the place."

Washington nodded. He agreed perfectly with this. But he was not sure that Trent, with a handful of men, could withstand the French if they decided to take over this site.

The governor seemed to read the officer's thought. "Don't worry. I'm sending Colonel Joshua Fry with a larger force to support Trent. And you, sir, who have learned a good deal about that region, are to accompany the colonel."

So Washington, promoted to lieutenant colonel, set out northwest again, this time in command of a company of Virginia militia. The orders he carried were brief and definite: "See that the fort on the Ohio is constructed and destroy or take prisoner any who oppose you."

The Virginians reached the post on Will's Creek without difficulty. There Colonel Fry was fatally injured and the young lieutenant colonel took over the command. It was a responsible position and a dangerous one. Here the Virginians learned that the French had, indeed, sent down a fleet of canoes to attack the fort which Captain Trent had started to erect. They had easily driven out the British and were in command of the site. They were completing the post and calling it Fort Duquesne.

This was the first open act of war in what was to be a long and bloody conflict. Washington knew that he and his men were in for a fight if they carried out their orders.

But the British force was small — about four hundred to stand against the thousands the French could send to fight them. Governor Dinwiddie had promised to send reinforcements, but so far none had come. Not wanting to wage a losing battle, Washington decided to wait a few days at Will's Creek for the promised help.

Spring rains had soaked the ground. The swampy lowland was a morass of quagmires. The streams were overflowing. The young commander sent out a force of workmen to widen and drain the road from Will's Creek toward the Monongahela. His troops would have to march this way if they retook the fort from the French.

This was the first crew of real road-builders to work on this twenty-mile stretch of old trail. The men had a tough job to do. Trees must be felled and underbrush grubbed out. Swamps must be drained and filled in; bridges constructed over swollen streams. And all this must be done while the rain poured down. These road-builders have been called the "greatest wielders of the ax the world has ever known."

The men were poorly clothed and scantily fed, yet they worked willingly, for their young commander inspired them. He did not sit in a dry tent while they labored in the rain. He was always out among them, showing by example what must be done. He was patient and considerate of his men, but he was growing more and more impatient at the delay. At last, when no troops had come from Virginia, he decided to set out with the men he had.

Slowly, with great difficulty and hardship, the wet and hungry troops marched along the narrow road. It was scarcely wide enough for the supply wagons, which bounced and jounced over stumps, rocks and underbrush. Rain soaked the men. Brambles tore their clothes and their flesh. When the road became too steep for the horses, the men pushed and pulled the heavy vehicles up the slopes. When there was a sheer drop, they fastened ropes about the wagons and around their bodies to hold back the wagons. Everyone worked, with Washington right among them, lending a hand whenever necessary. And he worked with eyes and ears alert, for he knew that hostile Indian and French spies lurked in the dark shadows of the forest, watching his every move.

Washington had his own scouts out. When the Virginians reached the Great Meadows, between the Youghiogheny and the Monongahela, these scouts warned the commander that a French party was approaching.

Washington, a surveyor and a soldier, knew that he was in a very poor place to take a stand. But there was no time to retreat. He must hastily throw up some sort of defense. And there was a slight advantage — the open ground would let them see any approaching force. There was also a good stream which would provide water. On the other hand, Laurel Hill on the south rose above the meadow. If the French chose the hill, they could shoot right down into any fort he might erect. But there was nothing else to do. Washington ordered a palisade to be thrown up, and his horses, supplies and troops were hastily brought into the scanty shelter. Because he had been compelled to erect the fort here, Washington grimly named it Fort Necessity.

The scouts reported that the French force was small and the commander decided that the best defense was offense. He would sally out and meet the enemy, instead of waiting to be attacked. He did this, and in a fifteen-minute battle, the Virginians killed a great many of the French, including their commander, Coulon de Jumonville. They also took twenty-one prisoners. So, in the first pitched battle of what came to be known as the French and Indian War, the Colonial troops, under their young commander, were victorious.

As soon as this skirmish had been successfully ended, Washington ordered his troops to march on. He had been sent out to retake Fort Duquesne and he meant to do so. He had not gone far when a force of some thousand French troops with Indian allies swooped down upon the Colonial soldiers. Washington had barely four hundred men. There was nothing to do but hastily retreat to Fort Necessity.

It was July 3 when the French attack on the frail little fort began. Rain fell steadily from a low sky. The Virginians stood in muddy trenches, their clothing soaked, the rain beating against their grim faces. The French had mounted Laurel Hill; their bullets and Indian arrows pelted straight down upon the beleaguered Colonials. As usual, Washington was out there in the rain and mud with his men.

All day long the fighting went on. As darkness fell, the French offered to parley. Washington decided that they were afraid that reinforcements would come up and attack their rear. They might better quit while they had the upper hand. But Washington had given up hope of help. He knew that to continue the fight would be to have his entire force wiped out. He didn't intend to let the French know of his desperate situation. Haughtily, he surrendered. But not without honor.

Washington demanded that his troops be allowed to march

away with all the honors of war, and with all their animals, stores and baggage. So, the next morning, July 4th, with flags flying and drums beating, the Colonial troops marched out of Fort Necessity. The victorious French had lost three hundred killed or wounded. The defeated Virginians had lost thirty killed and seventy wounded.

The twenty miles of road which Washington's men had improved so that wagons could travel over it, became known as Washington's Road. It played an important part in events that followed.

As news of the French attack spread through the colonies, the need to drive out these intruders became a grim determination. For a time it looked as if the colonies might unite under a common government in order to defeat the French. Benjamin Franklin worked out a constitution for such a union. But the colonies were fiercely jealous of their individual laws and customs. Most of them did not want to join into one government.

Then assistance came from England. An army under General Edward Braddock was sent to help the colonies defeat the French and save the rich Ohio Valley for King George II. Braddock was placed in command, also, of all Colonial forces.

The people were wild with enthusiasm, and began to flock to serve in the campaign. A popular song swept the country:

> To arms! To arms! my jolly grenadiers!
> Hark, how the drums do roll along!
> To horse! To horse with valiant good cheer;
> We'll meet our proud foe before long.
> Let not your courage fail you;

Be valiant, stout and bold.
And it will soon avail you,
My loyal hearts of gold.
Huzzah! my valiant countrymen — again I shout huzzah!
'Tis nobly done, the day's our own. Huzzah! Huzzah!

General Braddock looked at these shouting frontiersmen and his lips curled in contempt. He stripped the rank from every Colonial officer. Many refused to serve under him. Even George Washington resigned his commission. Later, seeing that the country needed him, he rejoined the militia and was sent to serve with Braddock. The general was now at Will's Creek, where the little post had been enlarged and renamed Fort Cumberland, in honor of the general's friend, Lord Cumberland.

In spite of his scorn for the Colonial soldiers, the general was glad to have Washington's help. He made the young officer his aide. He often asked Washington's advice, but seldom took it. At one time when the Virginian tried to warn Braddock about his treatment of their Indian allies, the general grew very angry. He shouted, "It's high time when Colonial buckskin can teach a British general how to fight!"

Washington had good reason to be concerned. The British troops were dressed as if for parade in London, not for battle in a swampy backwoods. Their light boots, buff-colored trousers, crimson lapels on jackets that gleamed with gold braid were not suitable attire for this wild country. The gaily bedecked drummer boys outshone the Colonial officers in their sober blue or stained buckskin. But General Braddock insisted that every man be in full and resplendent uniform.

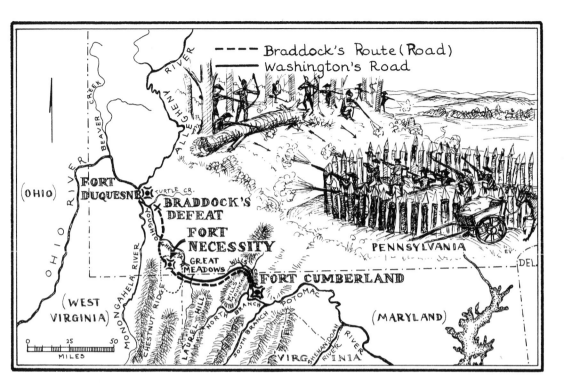

Of course Braddock knew that he could not really make a surprise attack on Fort Duquesne. The ring of ax on tree trunk, the blare of trumpets, the roll of drums, the neighing of horses and the shouts of men filled the woods with clangor. Even if the French had been deaf, the wide swathe being cut through the dark trees could not be overlooked. And at night the flare of camp fires lit up the sky for miles. Braddock had some two thousand men marching toward Fort Duquesne and he was aware that the French knew this.

Washington was not only worried, he was sick. For several days he had scarcely known whether he would outlive the journey. Now he rode among his men, so weak that a pillow was strapped to his saddle to support him.

By July 9, 1755, the British were just two miles from the Monongahela and twelve miles from the fort. Braddock laid out his plan of attack. His men would advance in full military formation along a narrow lane with a high, tree-covered ridge on one side and a deep gully on the other. They would take the fort in approved military fashion.

The French had no hope of holding their post against the British force, but they meant to do what they could. When they saw the enemy approaching in close formation they gave a shout of glee and turned their Indian allies loose. The British came on, closely packed, their scarlet ribbons, gold epaulets and shining muskets making bright targets against the dark green of the forest. French bullets and Indian arrows had no trouble hitting such a glittering quarry.

As soon as the Colonial troops saw what was happening, they broke rank and ran for cover behind trees. From this safety, they coolly returned the French fire. A few British soldiers followed this example, but General Braddock was furious at seeing his men fight like Indians. He ordered them back into line. He even struck with the flat of his sword one Virginian who did not obey promptly.

Bullets and arrows were coming from every direction. In the panic and confusion, British soldiers were even shooting into their own ranks. General Braddock had five horses shot down under him. Each time he quickly mounted another and rode on, ahead of his men. He seemed to have no fear, only anger at the stampede. Once he asked Washington what he should do. "Retreat, sir! Retreat!" the Virginian yelled. But General Braddock could not think of retreating.

Washington leading his men in the Battle of the Monongahela, in which General Edward Braddock was defeated.

All this time Washington was in the midst of the fighting, encouraging his men, urging them to take cover and answer ambush from ambush. Twice his horse fell, mortally wounded. Four bullets pierced his coat, but not one struck the young officer.

Finally a bullet hit the general. He fell among the pounding hooves, fatally wounded. Washington rushed to his aid, got him placed upon an abandoned cart and taken away from the dreadful scene.

The British and Colonial troops, bitterly defeated, managed to

Indians attacking from ambush the British under General Braddock.

escape back to their own fort. Braddock died on the fourth day after the battle. He was buried beside the rough road his men had built. George Washington read the brief burial service over the general's grave.

The French did not pursue their victory. They returned to Fort Duquesne confident that they had proved their right to the land. The Indian allies robbed the corpses. Decked out in the plumes and gold braid of the slain British, they danced and feasted in gleeful triumph.

Braddock's defeat was a terrible blow to the Colonists. But they were not entirely vanquished. Stronger than ever was the determination to recover the Ohio country. Three years later, Fort Duquesne would fall to the Colonial forces and would be renamed Fort Pitt.

The twelve-foot-wide path that Braddock's men had hacked through the forest and over the mountains from Fort Cumberland to the Monongahela — the first part of it an improvement of Washington's Road — was long known as Braddock's Road. Later, it

Trace of Braddock's Road still to be seen near Fort Necessity.

U.S. National Park Service

would become a segment of the National Road. So well done was the work of these early builders that traces of their labor may still be found in the forest between the Youghiogheny and the Monongahela. In some places one may still discover some of the great blocks of stone Braddock's men laid down to make a firm bed over which the heavy artillery wagons could pass.

And even today, according to the talk of old folks, on a quiet July evening the gleam of camp fires is seen on the hills, and the roll of drums and the rattle of gunfire can be heard.

Marker indicating Braddock's grave. The paved road at the left is a segment of U.S. 40, which here rather closely follows the road laid down by Braddock's men.

U.S. National Park Service

4

MAIL BY HORSEBACK

One autumn day in 1795 Colonel Ebenezer Zane leaned across the heavy oak table in his living room. His two younger brothers, Jonathan and Silas, were listening eagerly.

"It can be done! I've proved that! And it must be done. There must be an overland route to the settlements farther west. The river has served its purpose. But it is unpredictable, as you know. Floods, debris, snags, storms — all nature works to hinder travel on the river —"

"It has done well enough all these years," Jonathan began. His brother shook his head.

"Not well enough. How many boats have overturned within sight of this house? How many cargoes have gone to the bottom? Yes! How many lives have been lost on this untrustworthy Ohio?"

Silas grinned. "The French called it *La Belle Rivière* — the beautiful river. And you thought it that, yourself —"

Ebenezer nodded. "It is a beautiful river, but treacherous." Into his eyes, under their shaggy brows, came the look his brothers had often seen — the "westering look" they called it. It was in the eyes of the men who came floating down river on barges or flatboats or in canoes. It had always been in Ebenezer's eyes.

Sitting there in the colonel's comfortable living room, the brothers were remembering how, some twenty-five years earlier, Ebenezer had persuaded them to leave their good home on the south branch of the Potomac River to follow him north and west, seeking a fairer land. They had followed the old Seneca Trail through the woods and over the mountains and streams, and along the Great Warrior's Road searching for the land Ebenezer dreamed of. And here, on the Ohio, where Wheeling Creek entered the river, they had found it.

They remembered how their brother had stood on the brow of Wheeling Mountain, his eyes alight as he gazed down on the river with its forested banks, and its island, lush with grass and trees.

"It's like a vision of Paradise!" Ebenezer had said.

The years since had been filled with happiness and excitement. There were always the boatloads of travelers seeking a night's rest and food and shelter. From Virginia and Pennsylvania and Massachusetts they came — up the Potomac and the Monongahela, or by the Susquehanna and the Allegheny, to the fork of the Ohio. Then down the great river, seeking new homes, new fortunes. A few came on foot, through the dark forest along old Indian trails or over the traces hewed out by traders or soldiers. Remnants of these traces — paths wide enough for a horse but not for wagons — may still be found in many wooded areas of the Middle West and the South.

But travelers were not the only source of interest. There had always been the hazard of an Indian attack. The Mingoes had called this spot "Weeling" — the place of the skulls. Then, after their chief, Logan, went on the warpath, the region was still more dangerous. Logan had been friendly, but changed when his family was murdered by white soldiers. Fort Pitt, the scene of many a fray, was only some sixty miles up river by the trace Ebenezer had hacked through the forest to the outpost. Echoes of the troubles at the fort came down river to the Zanes. And during the Revolution, a fortified post had been erected here with Ebenezer in command. Life here had never been dull.

The wandering thoughts were brought back to what Ebenezer was saying. "You know that many movers, the families going west, would rather trust the dangers of the forest than the hazards of the river. It's easier to fight Indians and wild animals than it is to struggle against the snags and currents of the Ohio. These movers don't need a wagon road; a trace, a horse trail is enough.

"I know it's possible to hew out such a trace. My recent trip was to make sure of this. It could follow the Great Warrior's Road to the Muskingum; then southwest to the Hocking and from there south to the Scioto. Across that river it's just a short distance to Maysville in Kentucky. Already that is a busy settlement. The cargoes that pass here daily on the river are unloaded at Maysville to be shipped farther into the interior."

He had his brothers' attention, but he could read indecision in their eyes.

"There aren't many settlers along the route, but more will come. The road I plan would shorten the distance from here to Maysville by a hundred miles! And it could be traveled all year long. No snags, no floods, no whirling debris to upset one's belongings. Only the three rivers to be crossed —"

"And you'd build bridges?" Silas asked.

"No. I'd establish ferries. I picked out places where this could be done. And around the ferries settlements would soon grow up — with stores to sell food and clothing to the movers; blacksmith shops, harness makers, wagoners — everything needed for a prosperous town. I'd offer free lots to men who follow a needful trade —"

"You'd offer! You are rich, brother, but not that rich. Even you cannot afford such a grand project."

"I would not undertake it alone. As I rode along through the woods I worked out my plan. I would petition Congress to give me the authority to construct the road. In payment, all I'd ask would be a tract of land at each ferry site. That land I'd lay out into a town — sell lots —"

The younger men shook their heads. Land speculation! That was a sure way to lose money. How many land companies had already lost everything their promoters owned?

Ebenezer brushed away their gloomy thoughts. "I shall not lose. You'll see. Congress will grant my petition. I haven't mentioned my winning proposal. This road will serve the whole country —"

"How?" Silas asked briefly.

"As a mail route! You know how the mails are today, brought by boat. No one can tell when they will come in. Delayed by flood or storm — almost impossible to get up river during the winter. But over my road the mail could be carried by horseback on regular and definite schedules. And far more cheaply than now. Why" — he struck the table with his palm — "now the government spends four thousand dollars a year — hires fifteen men and their boats, to carry mail to the interior and out. Over my road it would cost a thousand dollars or less. Let me point this out to Congress, and I'll get my authorization to build the road and my tracts of land!"

Ebenezer was right. He sent his petition to Congress in March of 1796, and found many members interested in his plan. The soon to be elected Vice-President, Thomas Jefferson, was enthusiastic. Like Washington, Jefferson had long been thinking of the West and what would be needed to make it a vital part of the nation. Thousands of families were leaving the "crowded" East to seek new homes. Already Kentucky had been admitted to the Union, the first state west of the Alleghenies. Soon there would be enough people in Ohio to demand statehood.

There were also thousands settling in the Western Reserve. This was a huge section of land north and west of the Ohio River. It had been set aside — reserved — by Congress to provide homes for soldiers who had lost their property during the Revolution. The forward-looking, or westward-looking, members of Congress enthusiastically granted Ebenezer's petition.

Colonel Ebenezer Zane was authorized to start work on his trace. He was also given the tracts of land he had asked for. Each one was to be not more than a mile square.

Zane began with his usual energy. Actually, he had already started work before Congress had passed on his petition. Into the woods he sent his crews of axmen to fell trees, grub out underbrush and stumps, and widen the narrow trail he had followed on his trip to look over the possibility of making such an overland path to the South. Colonel Zane himself went along to oversee the work. With him were his brother Jonathan and his brother-in-law, John Mc-Intyre.

The work party traveled light. Supplies were loaded onto pack mules, as no carts could be taken over the trail. Tents would protect them from the weather and such necessary foods as sugar, flour, salt and bacon were taken along. They would find plenty of game and wild berries, and even honey. They were always on the alert against an Indian attack. For, although there was not much trouble now with the natives, it was impossible to predict when some grievance would set them against the white intruders.

All day long the forest rang with the sound of the axes as they bit into the hard boles of oak and walnut. For a while the woodsmen followed close along the northern bank of Wheeling Creek. Then they hacked their way up the mountain ridge and down the western slope. Here they found where coal could be dug out of the hillside for the forges of the blacksmiths in the party. Then they moved along the old Mingo Trail, always pushing westward.

At the Muskingum, where Licking Creek entered the river, Zane laid out his first town. Ebenezer was eager to push his trace on to Kentucky, so he gave this site to his brother and brother-in-law. They named the new settlement Zanesville, and a few years later when Ohio became a state, it was for a time the capital.

Ebenezer continued pushing his trace south and west. It was just a narrow path through the forest. The ancient trees walled it in deep shadow; the roots and stumps of those cut down stood axle-high. It was fetlock-deep in mud during the rainy months, and still deeper in dust during the dry season. But it was a trace over which horsemen could travel.

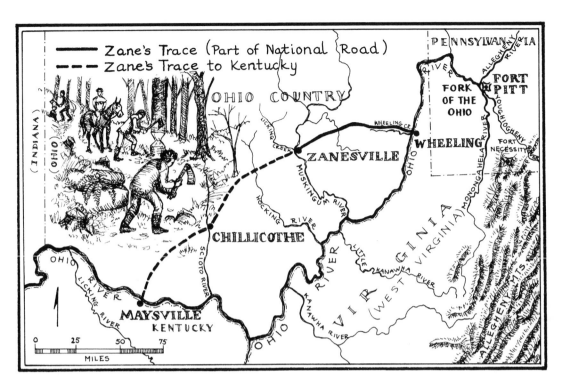

And it was traveled. Before it was anywhere near completion, it became the mail route from the interior of the country. As Ebenezer had predicted, the schedules became more settled; service was faster and more regular and far cheaper. The government had made a good bargain and Ebenezer Zane had planned well. In time wagons would use the trace after William Craig drove the first one over the stumps and rocks.

The part of Zane's Trace from Zanesville to Kentucky belongs to another story. The first segment, however, from Wheeling to

Zanesville became a section of the National Road. As folks made their way over it, always looking toward the great, open West, they lightened their long journey with song. A favorite was the "Chant for Overland Movers":

> Droop not, brother, as we go
> Over the mountains, westward, ho!
> Under the boughs of mistletoe
> Log huts we'll rear,
> While herds of deer and buffalo
> Furnish the cheer.
> File over the mountains, steady, boys.
> For game afar
> We have our muskets ready, boys,
> Aha!

5

TO BIND THE NATION TOGETHER

Lanky, sandy-haired Thomas Worthington dismounted from his tired horse and stood looking at the sorry cabin in front of him. Dogs, pigs, chickens and children had littered the yard with refuse and filth. The walls had been slapped together with little care; the door hung askew on leather hinges.

The wealthy Ohioan sighed and turned to his companion, a young Negro servant.

"Well, here we are at Peter Golly's. I detest stopping here, but stop we must."

He tossed his reins to the boy, who had also dismounted, and strode to the door. He rapped with irritation, well knowing that it would be opened by a slovenly woman. His evening would be spent among a flock of dirty, lazy, unkempt children; his supper almost inedible; his night would be misery on a hard pallet infested with vermin. Golly's was the worst stop on the road from Chillicothe,

59

Ohio, to Washington, D. C., but there were many others not much better.

"This must be changed," he told himself. "It is ridiculous to expect us to travel for two months over roads such as we have, staying in filthy cabins at night, in order that we may play our part in national affairs." Worthington, as a representative in Congress from the new state of Ohio, was on his way to the national capital to work for those things that would benefit his state, and so, he believed, would be good for the whole nation.

It was no wonder, he thought gloomily, that many Ohioans had opposed statehood. General Arthur St. Clair, the former governor of Ohio Territory, had been one of those who firmly believed it would be wiser to set up their own government in the West, with its capital closer to their settlements. But Worthington had worked for a unified nation. Four years earlier he had made this same journey to Washington to urge statehood for his adopted region. He was a Virginian by birth, but had moved west and now called Ohio his home.

Now here he was, with several days' journey still before him. It was a long and difficult trip along Zane's Trace — from Chillicothe to Zanesville and Wheeling, over the Ohio at Wheeling Cross and then on the old Cumberland Road on which Braddock and Washington had worked, to Cumberland. Now he would take the southern fork of the road east, to end up at Washington.

Thomas Worthington did not begrudge the time, expense and discomfort of the trip, so long as he was laboring for the good of the country. But he well knew that a good road would make it easier for others to take part in national affairs. Such a road would do more than anything else to bind the nation together into one unified whole.

As he tossed on the filthy pallet, he considered the struggle that lay ahead. He would have powerful allies: the President himself, for one. Thomas Jefferson had long believed that the country clear to the Pacific must one day come under a single flag. With this in mind, he had sent out, two years ago, an exploring party under captains Meriwether Lewis and William Clark. This expedition had not yet returned, but it was expected back in the fall. Whatever it had to report, Worthington felt sure, it would only strengthen the desire for a good road to the West.

There was Albert Gallatin from Pennsylvania, the Secretary of the Treasury, who was an enthusiastic supporter of the idea of a great highway westward. William Giles of Virginia could be counted on. And one of the most valuable supporters of the plan, Henry Clay of Kentucky, would use all his powers of oratory to win the day. These and others should be able to out-argue their opponents, but Worthington did not underestimate the weight of the objections to the undertaking.

"A description of this one stopping place," he thought drowsily, "ought to convince them. Or an account of the tree stumps and underbrush and rocks, of the mud and the chuck holes. I'll describe this one stopping place — that should open their eyes. Ohio and the rest of the West are too valuable to be lost through neglect."

The representative from Ohio found that the opposition to the road was every bit as powerful as he had imagined. Many of the Congressmen did not believe Congress had the right to use Federal money for such a project. And Federal help was what Worthington was fighting for. Rich as Ohio was in land, it did not have the money to build this road. Those who opposed the plan on the grounds that

Henry Clay used his powerful oratory to win support for the National Road. Here he is addressing the U.S. Senate.

it was unconstitutional were honest in their interpretation of the powers given to Congress. Many others, however, were against the project for purely selfish reasons. They did not want to see one part of the country "favored" by the national government, even though the whole nation would benefit indirectly.

The debates were often bitter, but at last those in favor of the Road won out. One big problem — how to pay for it — had been settled by the act that let Ohio become a state. This act provided that lands owned by the national government would be sold to settlers. Out of every hundred dollars cleared from such sales, five dollars would be set aside to pay for the Road.

Now, in March of 1806, Congress passed and the President approved a bill which provided for the construction of a Federal interstate highway. This bill has been called one of the most important ever passed by the Congress of the United States, for it meant that money collected from all states could be used for improvements in selected areas, even though some of the states might not benefit directly from the expenditure.

President Jefferson named a committee to plan the Road and to see that work began. On this committee were Thomas Moore and Eli Williams of Maryland and Joseph Kerr of Ohio. By January 31, 1807, these men had made their report to the President.

They began by pointing out that the committee realized the importance of a "road cementing the union of our citizens located on the Western Waters with those of the Atlantic States." Then they outlined the route the road should follow.

It was important to have the road go west in as straight a line as possible. This would save time, effort and money. It should pass through as many state capitals as possible in order to bind the seats of local government to the national capital and to make travel between them easier.

With these two objects in mind, they planned to start the Road at Cumberland, Maryland. The old fort on Will's Creek had grown into a bustling community. Good roads connected it with Baltimore and Washington and other eastern cities.

From Cumberland, Nemacolin's Wilderness Path, Washington's Road and Braddock's Road would be followed to the Monongahela. Here the new route would leave the river, to go up through a pass in the Alleghenies, down the western slope to the Ohio and across to Wheeling, Virginia (now West Virginia). From Wheeling it would be built along Zane's Trace to Zanesville, then due west to Columbus, Ohio. Eventually, it was hoped, the road would reach St. Louis, Missouri. At the eastern end, it would meet with roads coming up from Baltimore and Washington, D. C.

The roadbed was to be eighty feet wide. In the center, a strip thirty feet wide was to be covered with a layer of broken stone, a foot thick. On top of this would be a layer of gravel. It should be such a highway that all sorts of vehicles could use it, from passenger stagecoaches to the great Conestoga wagons.

Never in all the world, since the great days of road-building by the Romans, had any government undertaken to construct such a highway. The idea caught the imagination of the people all over the country. No matter where they lived, they took great pride in the project. This would be a highway fit for kings and emperors to travel over. This would bring the folks on the Ohio and Mississippi and Scioto and Kaskaskia within days of Washington, instead of months.

This S bridge on the East Pike (Road) in Ohio is similar to the bridge built in front of Lydia Shepherd's home on the National Road.

President Jefferson was so enthusiastic he predicted that people would be able to travel from Washington to St. Louis in six days. Actually, by 1837 this journey could be made in ninety-four hours, but as one could not travel continuously, but had to make stopovers, it required about ten days.

President Jefferson had said the road must go west in as straight a line as possible. But when actual construction began, it was found that there must be some "jogs" along the way. For one thing, sometimes it was easier and cheaper to go around a hill than to go over it. Such changes from the straight line were sensible.

But then some cities that found they would not be on the highway, though rather close, began to petition to have the road go a few miles north, or a few miles south in order to touch them. Uniontown, Pennsylvania, was one of these. And since this was the home of Albert Gallatin, who had worked so hard to make the road possible, Congress approved the change. Then the people of Washington, in the same state, thought the road should swerve down to pass through their town. This also was allowed.

Sometimes the reasons were not so logical. In West Virginia, on Middle Wheeling Creek, lived a charming young lady, Mrs. Lydia Shepherd. Lydia was a great friend of Henry Clay. She also loved company and had a beautiful home in which to entertain folks. She took a notion that the highway should go past her front door. She appealed to Mr. Clay, and since he had done so much for the road, he managed to grant the lady's request.

This made it necessary, however, to put a bridge across the creek at a place where a straight bridge could not be constructed. The result was a peculiar structure, almost in the shape of an *S*. This bridge is still to be seen. It stands as a monument to the persuasive ability of Mrs. Shepherd and to the genial good-nature of Henry Clay. And it may have been this bridge that caused some joker to declare:

Better, I vow,
If you can choose —
No bridge at all
'Stead of curlicues!

66

6

UNCLE SAM BUILDS A ROAD

Thomas Worthington had been delighted when Congress passed the bill authorizing the construction of a Federal highway. But as month followed month and piled up into years with scarcely any work being done on the project, he began to wonder if his labor had all been for nothing.

It had begun well enough. The very year the bill was passed a surveyor had been engaged. Josias Thompson set out, as young George Washington had done so many years before, from Cumberland on Will's Creek. As there was still nothing but primitive trails beyond the road built by Braddock's men, Thompson had to carry all his equipment and supplies on pack horses and mules.

Riding behind the surveyor and leading their pack animals came the crew. They were all taking this job very seriously. They had sworn that they would "faithfully and truly perform their duties as Chain Carriers while making a survey of this part of the United States Road."

These few men were the vanguard of the thousands who would have a part in the construction of the great highway. It took them two years to survey and mark the route from Cumberland to Brownsville on the Monongahela, a distance of about seventy-five miles.

But what miles they were! Forests, swamps and rivers and mountains blocked their way. The mountains were the biggest problem — Will's Mountain, fifty-eight hundred feet high and others two thousand feet and more. The surveyors must find a way that would not be too steep for a heavily loaded wagon. So, up the steeps and down the slopes the surveyors went, measuring distances, choosing grades, driving their stakes and pins to show just where the road must lie.

But although the surveyors had gone to work very soon after the bill was passed, it was five years before contracts were let for the actual road-building. In these years it seemed to Thomas Worthington, as to many others throughout the country, that Uncle Sam's Road would never be laid. But at last, in 1811, David Shriver was hired as superintendent of construction at a salary of $1,800 a year. He, in turn, employed subcontractors and laborers, and the actual work began.

First came the axmen to fell trees and grub out stumps and underbrush, and the haulers to drag them away. This was slow, hard work, especially along the first part of the road where the ancient trees had never felt the bite of an ax and the undergrowth had never been molested. Even where Washington and Braddock had laid down their roads there was still much to be done, for Uncle Sam's Road must be wider, smoother and less steep than the old military route had been.

After trees, stumps and underbrush had been removed, the roadbed must be leveled with pick and shovel. Hills had to be cut down, and the extra dirt and rock hauled away to fill up hollows and swamps.

Then came the rock-breakers. This was the toughest job of all and was usually done by crews of sturdy Irishmen. These strong, hard-working emigrants played a major part in the construction of the Road, just as they were doing in the building of the Erie Canal. Their red-flannel underwear was almost a uniform. Their Irish wit and love of singing helped them get through the long hard day for which they were paid, probably, fifty cents and their keep.

Work began at dawn and ended at dark. For breakfast, dinner and supper they were given huge slabs of pie, great mugs of coffee and piles of potatoes, beans and side bacon. And for this payment they sat, legs spread apart, breaking stone. They wrapped rags around their left hands, which held the rocks steady, while their callused right hands swung the heavy sledges. To protect their eyes they wore metal guards with slits in them, for the gray dust rose in clouds to settle in ears and nostrils, on hair and shoulders. For the road base, the stone must be broken into pieces small enough to go through a ring seven inches across. The top layer was of gravel, or stone broken to pass through a three-inch ring.

Usually the men sang as they worked, the sound of hammer

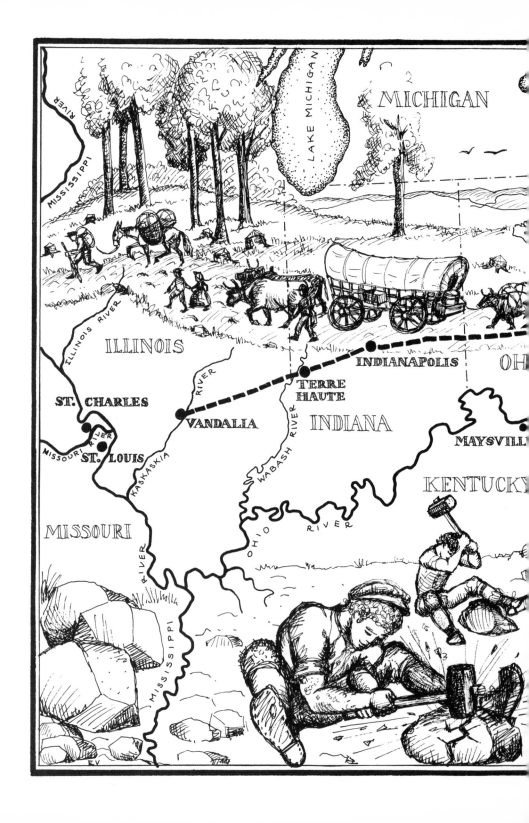

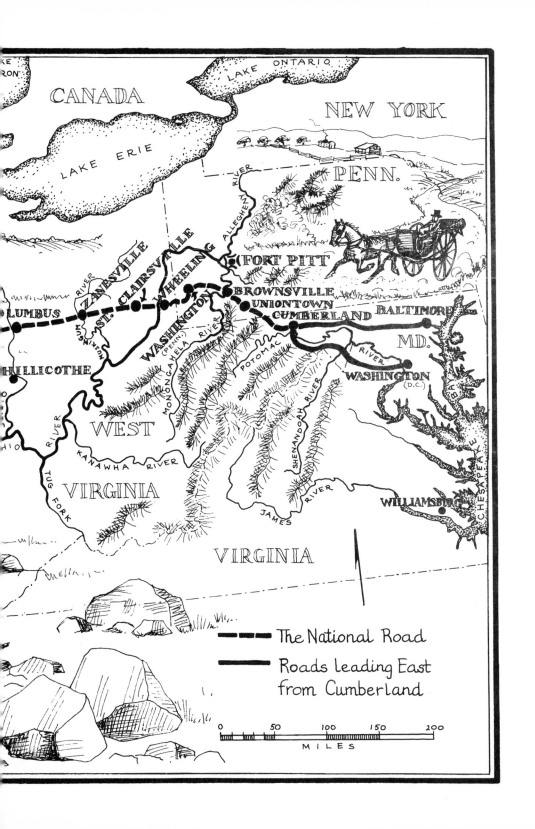

CANADA

LAKE ONTARIO

LAKE ERIE

NEW YORK

PENN.

RIVER

ALLEGHENY

ZANESVILLE

ST. CLAIRSVILLE

WHEELING

FORT PITT

BROWNSVILLE

UNIONTOWN

CUMBERLAND

BALTIMORE

...LUMBUS

MUSKINGUM RIVER

WASHINGTON (PENN.)

MONONGAHELA RIVER

POTOMAC

RIVER

MD.

...HILLICOTHE

RIVER

OHIO

WEST

KANAWHA RIVER

TUG FORK

VIRGINIA

SHENANDOAH RIVER

WASHINGTON (D.C.)

CHESAPEAKE BAY

JAMES RIVER

WILLIAMSBURG

VIRGINIA

- - - The National Road

——— Roads leading East
from Cumberland

0   50   100   150   200
MILES

against stone making a ringing accompaniment to their voices. Many of their songs were ballads brought over from their beloved Ireland, from which they had been driven by hard times and the harshness of the British government toward their homeland. But some were made up on the spot, and have become folk songs of the region through which the Road passed. So they sang:

> I came from Auld Ireland
>   Across the blue sea;
> And I dare any rocker
>   To break stone with me.
> I'm as brave as a lion,
>   As strong as an ox;
> And I cut my eyeteeth
>   On these Savage Mountain rocks!

It had taken the surveyors two years to mark seventy-five miles of route. It took the road builders that long to complete ten miles with some work on the next eleven miles. Immediately, even before the work was done, folks began to travel the new highway.

Along the Road, "fit for an emperor or king," rolled the great white-topped Conestogas of the families moving west. These wagons first appeared in the Conestoga Valley of Pennsylvania about the year 1750. For more than a hundred years they were the favorite vehicles of westering families. A Conestoga was a huge, cumbersome affair, with wide, heavy wheels that left deep ruts in the land they traversed. The wagon bed was constructed so that it was higher at each end than in the middle. This kept the load from spilling out on steep uphill or downhill slopes. The white wagon top had the same sway, only more pronounced. This gave the vehicle an unmistakable look. The main body of the wagon was always painted a bright blue; the upper woodwork and trim were always bright red.

These wagons often weighed more than three thousand pounds. It took a team of four or six horses, or of several oxen, to draw them. The horses were strong, tough animals and their owner decorated their bridles with tassels of red yarn. Above their heads arched a glittering brass frame to which small bells were attached. These jingled gaily as the wagon creaked along.

The Conestogas were always heavily loaded with chests and trunks and boxes, and with women and children. Crates holding chickens and geese were fastened to the sides; cows were tethered to the endgate. The men walked beside the ox teams, driving them with a long, sharp-pointed stick called a goad. Or they rode on the high, bright red seats above the sweating horses.

The bells added a merry note to the general confusion on the new Road. Men were still working along the sides of the highway, or, if their work was done, they would be moving tents and equipment to a new location. There were the shouts of drivers, the neighing of horses and braying of mules and barking of dogs and crying of children. There would be the jangle of harness parts, the creaking of wheels, and, far ahead the sharp ring of ax blade on tree trunk, or the shattering pound of sledge on stone.

It was wonderfully exciting to make a trip on the great Road, and travelers took the noise and confusion and inconvenience all with good spirit. After all, that was the best highway in the country, and would end all too soon. As the wagons rolled along, parents pointed out to children the historic sites they were passing: Fort Necessity, Braddock's Grave, the scenes of the historic battles along the route.

Three more years passed before the next eighteen miles to the Youghiogheny River were done. By 1818, seven years after the first contracts were given, the Road was over the hill on the east bank of the Ohio. Now it moved swiftly down to the river, across which lay Wheeling, where, nearly fifty years earlier, Ebenezer Zane had built the first house and store. Now there were a dozen stores and many very good houses to accommodate the hundred and twenty families that lived there, and the flocks of movers that stopped overnight on their journey west.

Work on the Road bogged down at Wheeling, and for a time it seemed as if this might be the end of the famous project. But the people just could not let this happen. At Wheeling they looked toward the West and longed for more of the great highway instead of the narrow, stump-filled, rutted road ahead.

Jefferson, of course, was no longer President, but most of those who followed him had seen to it that there was some money for the road. Henry Clay, "the idol of the West," was constantly urging that the highway be extended. So, in 1820 Congress set aside $10,000 for surveying the Road on from Wheeling to the Mississippi River at a point near St. Louis, Missouri. The first eighty-one miles, from Wheeling to Zanesville, would follow the trace hacked out by Ebenezer Zane and his men. Ten thousand dollars was not nearly enough money, even in those days, to construct such a road. It was not even enough to make a good start. So nothing was done for several more years.

Ever since 1776 the Fourth of July had been a great patriotic holiday for the people of the United States. But July 4, 1825, was an extra-special day in St. Clairsville, Ohio. Here, in the town named for the former governor, Arthur St. Clair, who had opposed the building of the National Road, a huge crowd was gathered. In front of the flag-bedecked courthouse the men, women and children listened to patriotic speeches, to the brass band playing stirring airs, to the hymns and anthems sung in honor of the day. They were celebrating not only the nation's birthday, but also the rebirth of the great Road. At last, work was to start on the highway across Ohio, Indiana, Illinois and Missouri. It would start right here at St. Clairsville.

From this day on, the story of the National Road is filled with contrast. There was jubilation as each new section was completed. There was happy hustle and bustle as wagons and pack trains moved over it, or droves of pigs, cattle or wild turkeys were driven along. There were the shouts of children, the yelled commands of drovers and the singing of the wagoners:

> We're coming, Ohio!
> We're coming, Ohio!
> Our six-horse team
> Will soon be seen
> On the road through Ohio!

The old State House at Vandalia, Illinois, was erected when Vandalia was the state capital and when the National Road was being constructed.

But there was also disappointment when Congress did not appropriate money; there were delays when work stopped for months. Sometimes the President and the Congress were not enthusiastic over the idea of a National Road and did nothing to help it along. But always there were Henry Clay and a few others pushing and prodding and keeping the Road alive.

Bit by bit, it crept on across Ohio from St. Clairsville to Zanesville over hills and twisting streams. From Zanesville to Columbus the land was flatter, but the work went slowly, and it was 1833 before the Ohio capital was reached.

By this time the people in the East were thinking about railroads rather than wagon roads. Why waste money on highways, they asked, when soon everyone would be traveling over shining iron rails? This made it more difficult to wangle money from Congress, but the people of Ohio, Indiana and Illinois did not stop asking. They had little faith in the newfangled trains; Conestogas and stagecoaches were more reliable.

Mail between East and West had grown to a tremendous volume. People in the West felt that just the mail alone was enough to warrant the completion of the National Road, to say nothing of the "movers" who were still using wagons and pack trains. But it would be 1850 before the Road reached Indianapolis, and two years later before it stopped at Vandalia, Illinois.

The farther sections of the Road were never as well constructed as the first sections. In some places the original specifications were somewhat followed. In others the rock-covered roadbed was abandoned. In the worst segments, no surfacing at all was done, and tree stumps and rocks were not removed. Only the path sliced through the trees showed where the road lay.

In a few places, small logs were cut and laid side by side across the path, making a corduroy road. This was strong, but very hard on horses and wagons. In other sections, the workmen used a method they had learned was quite common in Russia: to cover the roadbed

This painting depicts the laying of a plank road, such as was used on some parts of the National Road. This particular segment was laid between Columbia and Providence, Missouri.

with planks. But this was also hard on wagons and expensive to keep up.

A pleasing variation was brick paving. The dull red bricks, laid in patterns in several Ohio and other midwestern towns, are very attractive and have withstood the crunch of wheels and the pounding of hooves for more than a hundred years. Such roads would be too expensive to be constructed today.

Politics and lack of money halted the building of the National Road at Vandalia; it was not after all extended to St. Louis. But nevertheless the great Road, the National Road, was an actuality. The wisdom of buffalo and Indian, of young George Washington and crochety General Braddock, of Nemacolin and Ebenezer Zane had been proved.

7

LIFE ON THE NATIONAL ROAD

For some forty-five years, from about 1825 to 1870, the National Road was the great channel of travel and communication between the East and the West. Folks swarmed down from Vermont, Connecticut, Massachusetts and Rhode Island. They came from all parts of the South to join the throngs moving west.

But it was not only a route of travel: the National Road helped also to establish towns and cities throughout the interior of the country. Every few miles along the entire length of the highway, inns and taverns must be set up to care for the travelers. Soon stores, blacksmith shops, harness makers, stables appeared close to the inns. People came to manage these places, and built houses to live in. And there was a town.

Sometimes moving families heard of a "good place to settle" some miles north or south of the highway. They would turn their wagons away from the Road, and drive off to the fabled site. Some-

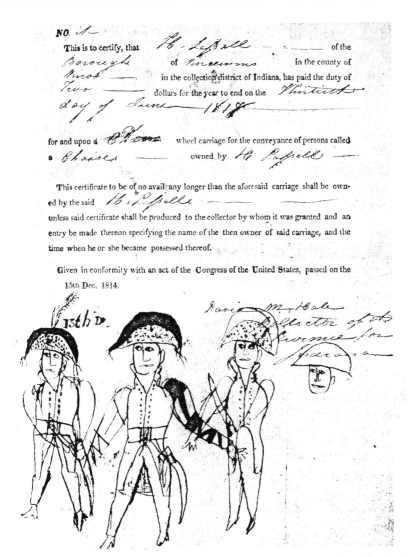

NO. 1

This is to certify, that *H. Leffell* of the

Borough of *Vincennes* in the county of

Knox in the collection district of Indiana, has paid the duty of

Two dollars for the year to end on the *Thirtieth*

day of *June* 1817

for and upon a *two* wheel carriage for the conveyance of persons called

a *Chaise* owned by *H. Leffell*

This certificate to be of no avail any longer than the aforesaid carriage shall be own-

ed by the said *H. Leffell*

unless said certificate shall be produced to the collector by whom it was granted and an

entry be made thereon specifying the name of the then owner of said carriage, and the

time when he or she became possessed thereof.

Given in conformity with an act of the Congress of the United States, passed on the

15th Dec, 1814.

15th D.

David M. Hale
Collector of the
Revenue for
Indiana

Indiana Historical Society

In 1817 a person had to have a license such as this one issued in Indiana for owning a chaise, or buggy. The cost was $2 a year. The soldiers were drawn in by some doodler.

times they were disappointed, but often the report had been true, and another settlement was started some distance from the Road.

While this was going on, fascinating sidelights were being added to the story of American life.

81

An example is the Irish workmen. Many of these lived for a time in tent towns or shanties along the Road they were building. Sometimes the shanties were not abandoned when the crew moved on. They became small settlements in which Irish names and Irish customs and legends still live today.

The Road made many people start living in a new way: the tavern keepers, the drovers and wagoners and the stagecoach drivers all had to forget the ordered ways of city life and adapt to the hustle and bustle and constant movement of the busy highway.

Aside from the Irish workmen, many of those who engaged in business along the highway were descendents of British immigrants. They had recently come from Europe and bore names which have disappeared, or have been changed somewhat to meet modern taste. Such names, once familiar along the Road, bring back a sense of the time: Ashkettle, Livingood, Manypenny, Noggle and Sidebottom are actual names once seen on tavern signs or store fronts in Ohio, Indiana and Illinois.

Washington and Jefferson had felt that such a road would "bind the nation together." They could not have foreseen how well it would do this job.

Travelers by the thousands poured over the Road. They carried with them the news and gossip and styles from eastern cities. During meals at the taverns they exchanged ideas, argued political questions, learned what each section thought and felt. The products of Ohio and other interior regions which had formerly gone down the Mississippi to New Orleans and the settlements along the river, now were sent to the factories in the East. Easterners began to depend on coal from the Ohio mines, on salt from the Kanawha Valley, on corn and

This is an early stage wagon, somewhat different from the later coaches used on the National Road.

beans from the Plains. At the same time, the settlers in the West were getting cloth and shoes and iron manufactured in the East. It was a give-and-take exchange made possible by the National Road.

Because of the Road new types of transportation were developed. The Conestoga wagon had long been used in Pennsylvania; now it became familiar to the entire country. The development of stagecoach travel was due to the Road. The first public conveyances had been used in the East. They were slow, cumbersome "stage wagons," sometimes sarcastically called "flying machines." They were very

A stagecoach barn on the old National Road in Indianapolis in the 1840's.

uncomfortable, with no springs. A traveler felt lucky to arrive at his destination all in one piece.

The first stagecoach over the National Road went from Cumberland to Wheeling in 1817. It was of the ugly, uncomfortable type. But as travel increased, stagecoach companies were formed. They began to compete with each other for the trade. They found that speed and comfort were the two things travelers wanted most. The company owners began to look for ways of meeting these demands. Gradually the curved roof of the coach was flattened, so baggage could be carried on top and so there was more head room inside. At first there were no steel springs and a traveler felt as if his spine must have been cracked by the jerks and jounces. Then the coach body was hung in a sort of leather swing. It was, perhaps, an improvement, but now the traveler swung back and forth and from side to side till he was dizzy.

The stagecoaches were painted in bright colors and given fanciful names such as the Flying Ace, Lafayette, or Western Star. The stagecoach companies also adopted names the owners felt would attract customers. One of the most famous was the June Bug Line. Because people were used to water travel, many sea terms crept into use. The owner of a stagecoach company was called a "land admiral." Conestoga wagons became "prairie schooners" or "land frigates."

The stagecoach usually had three seats, crosswise of the interior. Each seat held three passengers and an extra might ride up beside the driver. This place was generally liked during good weather. In-

A hundred years ago covered bridges spanned many a stream. Here a loaded coach of the early style comes dashing through such a bridge, probably on its way West.

Indiana State Library

More than one traveler is riding outside on this speedy coach carrying the U.S. mail. The six-horse team had to be one of the best.

side, those on the middle and back seats faced the driver; the ones in front faced the rear. In time, the seats were upholstered, but in spite of everything, the stagecoach was not any too comfortable.

Good horses and good drivers were necessary to insure speed. Each company tried to hire the very best. Montgomery Deming, who drove for the June Bug Line, was a huge fellow weighing almost five hundred pounds. He could drive his six-horse team at an average rate of more than five miles an hour. In emergencies he could make ten miles an hour. Such emergencies occurred when a Presidential message had to be delivered, or when a President-elect was in a hurry to get to the capital. Then the driver might roll along singing:

> A lead team,
> A wheel team,
> A very precious load —
> Taking the President's message
> Down the U.S. Road!

There were accidents on the Road, even in those days. Here a cart loaded with hay loses a wheel at Thornville, Ohio.

Century Magazine, July, 1891

Road accidents might occur at any time. Here oxen, worn out and dying of thirst, lie down and can go no farther.

Speeding along was dangerous and sometimes disastrous. A sharp curve, an unexpected rock, the sudden shying of a frightened horse might easily tip the coach over onto its side, dumping the passengers into the road. Among famous men thus dumped out were Martin Van Buren and Henry Clay. Neither man was seriously injured.

All the horses had names, and the names of the fastest became famous. Mambrino, Matchless, Hero and Patrick Henry were talked about from Cumberland to Springfield. Drivers were forbidden to race along the Road, but it was impossible to prevent them.

Every twelve miles or so was a relay station with fresh horses. The driver would swing up to the station, where the new team stood, harnessed and ready, beside the road. As soon as he came up, the driver threw down the lines. An attendant immediately unharnessed the incoming team and led it away. Another backed the fresh team up, adjusted the harness, tossed the lines up to the driver, and away went the coach. The change was made with such speed that the passengers scarcely realized it had been done.

Stagecoach passengers stopped at inns. An innkeeper was obliged to take in, feed and bed every person who came to his door wishing such accommodation. Since the road was heavily traveled — as many as twenty four-horse coaches could be counted on one section of the Road at busy times — the inns were often overcrowded. Sometimes

This picture shows a typical inn on the National Road, with a Conestoga drawn up in front, animals in the yard, and what may be a neighboring farmer with a load of slaughtered pigs.

Library of Congress

men were bedded down on the floor, so close together that there was no room to step between them. One traveler was awakened by a rooster crowing. He found that chickens had come in through the open door and had roosted on the foot of his bed.

The food was abundant and hearty, with whatever meat was handy as the main dish. Fried trout, roast venison, fried or stewed chicken, roasted wild turkey were common. Potatoes, beans, hot corn

A page from the daybook of the Union Inn in Indianapolis in 1833. It shows lodging and breakfast cost 37½ cents; dinner, 25 cents.

Indiana Historical Society

Cabins like this often were the only overnight stopping places on the old Road to Ohio.

bread and molasses or Indian pudding filled out the menu. Such a meal usually cost twenty-five cents; bed and breakfast might cost thirty-seven and a half cents.

In addition to the Conestogas and the stagecoaches, the road was crowded with pack trains of mules and with droves of sheep or pigs or turkeys. The wagoners and drovers did not stop at the inns. They spent their nights at "wagon stands" where there were stables and pens for their animals. Here they were with the kind of folks they knew and liked. The evenings could be spent in telling tall tales of

The following specification of the fare of the principal Stage Routes, by which the traveller may reckon the cost of his tour, will not be superfluous.

		Miles.	
From Philadelphia to Pittsburgh,		300	$15 00
Philadelphia	Baltimore,	128	3 00
Baltimore	Wheeling,	271	12 00
Pittsburgh	Wheeling	59	4 00
Wheeling	Columbus,	140	8 00
Columbus	Cleaveland,	177	10 50
Columbus	Chillicothe,	45	2 00
Chillicothe	Cincinnati,	94	5 50
Columbus	Cincinnati, direct,	110	6 50
Indianapolis	Madison,	86	4 00
Cincinnati	Lexington,	76	4 50
Lexington	Louisville,	75	4 50
Louisville	St. Louis, via Vincennes,	267	15 50
Louisville	Nashville,	180	12 00
Richmond	Cincinnati, via Staunton, Lewisburg, Charleston on the Kanhaway and Guyandot, thence 155 miles by steamboat,	515	28 00
Richmond to Knoxville, via Lynchburgh, Abington, Kingsport, &c.,		444	28 50
Baltimore to Richmond, via Norfolk, by steamboat,		378	10 00
Knoxville to Nashville, via McMinville,		119	12 50
Nashville	Memphis,	224	15 00
Nashville	Florence,	110	8 25
Huntsville	Tuscaloosa,	155	10 00
Florence	Tuscaloosa,	146	9 00
Tuscaloosa	Montgomery,	119	8 00
Tuscaloosa	Mobile, by steamboat,	676	12 00
Augusta	Montgomery,	300	18 50
Montgomery	Mobile	180	12 00
Mobile	New Orleans,	160	12 00
St. Augustine to New Orleans,		600	35 00
Boston and New York to New Orleans, by packet, cabin passage, fare inclusive, from			$40 to 50 00

This page from Warner's *Immigrant's Guide* shows the fares charged for stagecoach trips on the National Road in 1848.

their experiences, and in singing and dancing. While an inn might carry a sign such as:

> This gate hangs high
> And hinders none;
> Refresh and pay
> And travel on.

the wagon stand would boast of its service:

> Oats, corn and hay, I always have on hand,
> For plenty I always raise on my own land.
> And if I should keep two droves at once
> It wouldn't lower my oat bin much.

But wagons and coaches and droves of animals did not have the road to themselves. Always, there were the buggies of rich travelers, the carts of peddlers, the makeshift vehicles of those who could not afford the stage, even though the fare from Baltimore to Wheeling was only $17.25. And there were the walkers, trudging along, pack on back, sleeping by the roadside.

The National Road "woke up" at dawn. Animals were fed and watered, breakfast eaten, and bedding and utensils picked up and packed. Folks liked to start out early. Some did not stop to eat breakfast, but traveled on for a couple of hours before eating. This broke into the morning, gave the children a chance to stretch their legs and the animals a little time to rest.

All day long the stream of traffic flowed, mostly west, but eastward, too. The National Road was as busy and crowded for its time as today's freeways.

8

DANIEL BOONE HELPS OUT

The first persons to penetrate the unknown western lands were those adventurous traders who carried the white man's goods to the Indians and brought back furs. The settlements along the Delaware were established so that Sweden could share in such trade with the Indians. It was the British traders who first felt the attacks of the French. The French villages along the Mississippi were largely centers for such ventures.

Almost a hundred years before Ohio became a state, the little town of Kaskaskia was a busy community. It lay on the east bank of the Mississippi, in what would later become the state of Illinois. Some sixty miles south of where St. Louis would be, Kaskaskia, settled in 1703, is said to be the first settlement by Europeans in the West.

It was truly the frontier. Yet even here the people looked to the West — to the lands owned by Mexico and the trade that might be developed with the Mexican towns.

Year	Value of Merchandise	Wagons	Men	Remarks
1822	$15,000		70	Pack-animals only used.
1823	12,000		50	"
1824	35,000	26	100	" and wagons.
1825	65,000	37	130	" "
1826	90,000	60	100	Wagons only henceforth.
1827	85,000	55	90	
1828	150,000	100	200	3 men killed, being the first.
1829	60,000	30	50	1st U.S. Escort—1 trader killed.
1830	120,000	70	140	First oxen used by traders.
1831	250,000	130	120	2 men killed.
1832	140,000	70	150	Party defeated on Canadian.
1833	180,000	105	185	2 men killed, 3 perished.
1834	150,000	80	160	2nd U.S. Escort.
1835	140,000	75	140	
1836	130,000	70	135	
1837	150,000	80	160	
1838	90,000	50	100	
1839	250,000	130	250	Arkansas Expedition.
1840	50,000	30	60	Chihuahua Expedition.
1841	150,000	60	100	Texan Santa Fe Expedition.
1842	160,000	70	120	
1843	450,000	230	350	3rd U.S. Escort—Ports Closed.

Josiah Gregg included this table of the Santa Fe trade in his *Commerce of the Prairies*, published in 1844.

In 1804 a Kaskaskia merchant sent a French Creole named La Lande on an expedition to some of these settlements. La Lande went to Santa Fe, transacted his employer's business, pocketed the profit and never returned to report his success.

The following year another trader, James Pursley, ventured to

A very early sketch of St. Louis, Missouri, showing how close the buildings came to the riverside.

Santa Fe, and on farther west. When he came back to the Mexican pueblo he reported that he had found gold on the flank of Pike's Peak (which, of course, at that time did not have this name).

When the Mexicans heard of Pursley's discovery, they kept him in Santa Fe, trying to learn the exact site of the goldfield. It was in Mexican land, and they wanted to benefit from it. Pursley stubbornly refused to tell them where the place was. He claimed that since it had been discovered by an American, it belonged to the Americans.

The next year, Zebulon M. Pike was sent by President Jefferson into the Southwest to explore the borderland of this Mexican territory. He went as far as the peak which bears his name. On his way back he met Pursley, who confided his story to the officer. In this way, rumors of gold in the Pike's Peak region were circulated.

But how did Pursley and Pike and others get from the eastern settlements to the Southwest? They generally came down the Mississippi to some settlement, and from there set out westward. After St. Louis was established in 1764, it became the chief outfitting point for journeys to the West and Southwest. It was only natural then that when in 1825 Congress appropriated more money for building the National Road past Wheeling, it should select a point near St. Louis as the terminal. The original plan of having the Road go due west in a straight line had to be changed somewhat. From Terre Haute, Indiana, it would slant southwest to Vandalia, Illinois. This town was some sixty miles east of the place where travelers usually crossed the Mississippi River, just above St. Louis.

The people in the West were so eager to get the Road finished that work had been going on west of Indianapolis at the same time that more easterly sections were being constructed. This made it possible for the road from here to Vandalia to be completed even before sections farther east were finished. As travel increased, the capital of Illinois was moved from Kaskaskia to Vandalia. The statehouse built at this time is still standing. Later still, the capital was moved to Springfield, which does not lie on the National Road.

Gold is often said to be the magnet that drew thousands to the Far West. However, something far more necessary to life also did much to lure folks westward. This was salt, which was scarce in the East. Travelers were always looking for a salt lick — a place where buffalo and other wild animals came to get this needed mineral. When such a lick was found, the word spread rapidly. Many times

Harper's, June, 1887
Daniel Boone and his family marked the trail to Boon's Lick, Missouri.

a settlement grew up around the lick. This is shown in the names of some towns, such as Big Bone Lick, Kentucky.

Daniel Boone, canny frontiersman that he was, had once made his home near the salt springs on the Kanawha River in Virginia (now West Virginia). There he had "made salt" to sell to travelers. Now he would take a hand in building a path from St. Louis on westward.

DANIEL BOONE HELPS OUT

On the Missouri River, some hundred and thirty-five miles west of St. Louis were a group of salt springs which the Spanish government granted to Colonel Nathaniel Boone about 1799. Nathaniel was the youngest son of Daniel and Rebecca. When he was eighteen he married sixteen-year-old Olive Van Bibber. With his wife and his parents and his brother Daniel Morgan, he had moved into the Missouri country at the time the Spanish government was encouraging its settlement by Americans.

Nathaniel and his brother, with two companions, went to St. Louis in 1806 and bought a dozen twenty-gallon salt kettles. They returned to the springs and began making salt. They were so success-

Even after the advent of the automobile, Boon's Lick Trail was popular, as shown by this map which claimed that at Boonville was the only place cars could safely cross the Missouri River between St. Louis and Kansas City.

State Historical Society of Missouri

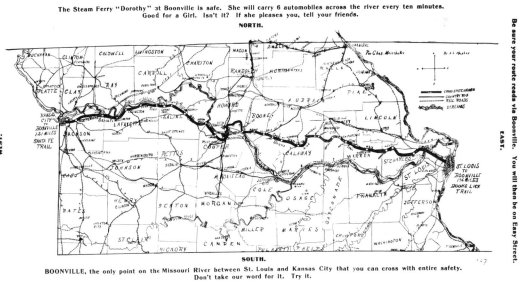

MAP—CENTRAL HIGHWAY LOG—ST. LOUIS—KANSAS CITY
(VIA BOONVILLE—THE SANTA FE AND BOON'S LICK TRAIL ROUTE)
n. d.

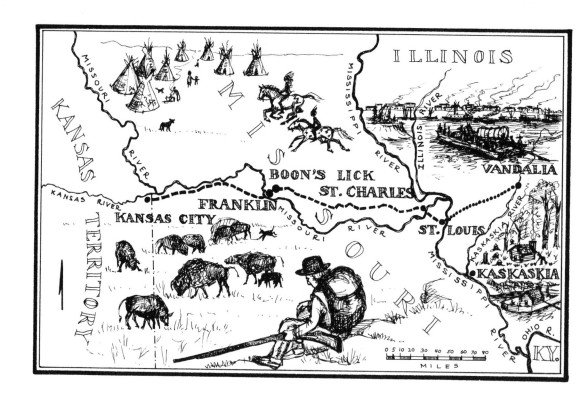

ful that the next year they purchased forty more kettles, employed six helpers, and produced a hundred bushels of salt a week.

Much of this was carried down to St. Louis to be sold. And, of course, folks going west made a little trip to the springs to lay in a supply of the needed mineral. The place became known as Boon's Lick, and the path to it was called Boon's Lick Trail. The trail ended a few miles farther on at the town of Franklin. This settlement was on the bank of the Missouri, just where the channel of the great river turns north for some distance.

Franklin was an important settlement in the early 1800's. From this point, fur trappers going to the Rocky Mountains and beyond, proceeded up the Missouri to its headwaters. And it was here that those making the journey to Santa Fe and other Mexican pueblos left the river to travel overland to the Southwest.

Many of the men whose names are famous in western lore knew Franklin. Kit Carson, born in Kentucky, was brought to Boon's Lick country when he was two years old. At nine he was apprenticed to a blacksmith in Franklin. It was from this blacksmith shop that Kit, at sixteen, ran away to join a Santa Fe caravan. Jedediah Smith, Jim Bridger, Tom Fitzpatrick and other great mountain men passed through the settlement either going to or coming from St. Louis.

Travelers to the West who came over the National Road to Vandalia would proceed on to the Mississippi. There they'd take the ferry across the river. Often the ferry boatman might chant:

> I'll hold her nose to the dock
> Till the last galoot's ashore!

From St. Louis, or St. Charles just to the northwest of the larger city, the westering folks would travel the Boon's Lick Trail to Franklin.

There they would say good-bye to civilization. Beyond lay the unsettled West with all its mystery and danger. Some would travel up the river to its headwaters. Others would go by wagon train or horseback due west toward the Rockies. Still others would turn southwest to face the dreadful desert with its sixty-mile "journey of death" on the road to Santa Fe. (See map on page 104)

Because of their part in making a trail west from St. Louis, the names of Daniel Boone and his family must join other noted names connected with the National Road; Nemacolin, Washington, Jefferson, Clay, Zane, Worthington, and others to come later. Significantly, Boonville, Missouri, is a thriving town today, situated directly upon the great Road to the West, and just a little more than a mile south of Franklin.

9

TO THE PACIFIC

On a hot midsummer day in 1827, three scarecrow figures came out of the desert to gaze in awe and rapture on the shimmering waters of the Great Salt Lake. The men were Jedediah Strong Smith, Silas Gobel and Bob Evans. They led two horses and a mule, mere skins filled with bones that could be counted through the sagging hides. They had been nearly a month making their way across the great American desert in what is now Nevada and western Utah.

Jedediah Smith was one of the greatest explorers of the Far West. A year before, he had left his trapper companions at Bear Lake and had set out for the Pacific coast. He had with him fifteen men and a train of horses and mules packed with goods to trade with any Indians he might meet along the way.

The party had taken a southern route and had reached California safely. There they had been taken prisoner by the Mexican officials, but had finally been permitted to leave if they would go immediately back to American territory. From the Stanislaus River,

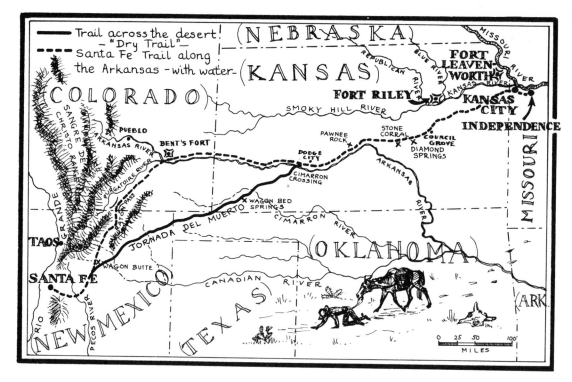

Trail across the desert! — "Dry Trail" —
Santa Fe Trail along the Arkansas - with water -

(See text, page 102.)

Jedediah and his men had made their way northeast toward the Sierras. But in midwinter they had been unable to cross the mountains. So they went into camp, until spring. In May, with only two companions, seven horses and two mules, the leader had again set out and made a successful crossing of the snow-covered heights.

It had taken them eight grueling days to get through the snow-filled passes of the Sierra Nevada Mountains. Twenty more days had been used in crossing the desert. There were no trails here — neither buffalo nor Indian had marked the way. If any had gone over this

104

ground before, the desert wind had swept loose sand to cover their footprints. This gallant trio was making their own path, with only the mountain man's instinct to guide them.

They emerged from the desert at the southwest corner of the Great Salt Lake. They traveled along the southern shore and turned north to rejoin their companions on Bear Lake. They were the first men known to have traversed this route south of the lake.

Years later, John Charles Frémont, guided by Kit Carson and Joseph Reddeford Walker, was looking for a shorter route to the coast than the old Oregon Trail. The party had left St. Louis that spring. They followed Boon's Lick and the Santa Fe Trail up the Arkansas, turned north to cross the Rockies by an easy pass, and then northwest to the Great Salt Lake. Frémont and Kit had done a little exploring of the lake two years before, coming down to it from the north. But the explorer wished to see it again.

Joe Walker, one of Frémont's guides on this journey, was familiar with most of the West. Long before this, he had led a party along the Humboldt River to the Sierras, a route followed by one or two emigrant trains after that.

Now, in 1845, Frémont camped on the south shore of the lake and while his men made salt from the briny water, the leader studied the westward scene. Ahead stretched a flat, treeless expanse of sand, without a tree to break the gray monotony. Frémont asked his guides, "Do you know anything about the route west from here?"

Kit shook his head. "Ain't nary a white man ever set his foot on that land. Injuns say no food, no water. Only death out thar."

But Frémont wasn't one to be deterred by Indian tales. He turned to Joe Walker, who shook his head. Kit was right; he explained. No one could travel between the lake and the river flowing west.

"Best way to git to that river is down from Fort Hall — not out this way," Joe said. "Come down from Fort Hall, you kin easy hit the stream. But 'twixt here and there —" He left the rest to his leader's imagination.

Frémont sent ahead an exploring party, which he followed with his mules laden with casks filled with fresh water. They crossed the desert without too much trouble, went over the Sierras and reached Sutter's Fort on the Sacramento. But they had not gone straight west. They had turned away from the Humboldt River, which Frémont named for a German naturalist he admired, to reach Walker's Lake and cross the mountains by the pass named for the guide.

A year later an emigrant party led by Lansford W. Hastings followed a route that ran for much of the way along Frémont's path. Later that year another party had a tragic experience when it attempted to go due west from the Great Salt Lake to California. This was a group led by James Frazier Reed and George and Jacob Donner. It became known as the Donner-Reed party.

These people turned south from the Oregon Trail to reach the Great Salt Lake. They camped on the bank of a river that emptied into the lake (the Jordan River). By now there were eighty-seven people in the party, most of them strangers to each other.

It was already September when they set out across the "salt mud" desert southwest of the Great Salt Lake. Here they were delayed by the gummy mud and by lack of water and fodder. Oxen fell exhausted; wagons had to be left and then later men turned back to rescue the vehicles. All across what is now Nevada they had trouble

An artist tried to show the suffering of the ill-fated Donner party in this illustration for an article in *Century* magazine, July, 1891.

Marshall's Discovery of Gold, California, January 19th, 1848. SUTTER'S MILL, 1851. Copyright Secured. From Nahl's Famous Paint Copyrighted 1876, by A. Rom

Sutter's Mill, on the South Fork of the American River (where Sacramento, California, now stands). Here, in January, 1848, the gold nugget was found which started the great Gold Rush of 1849.

and hindrances. There were quarrels and desertions. It was winter before they reached the Sierra Nevada Mountains.

They felt they must go on and started to climb into the forbidding heights. There, high in the mountains, just a hundred miles from the shelter of Sutter's Fort, terrific storms hit them. They could go no farther. They were forced to make a sort of camp here, where many died of cold and starvation, before they were rescued by men from Sutter's. Some lived through those desperate days by eating boots and harnesses and worse. Of the eighty-seven who started from the Jordan River, only forty-two were alive to be taken down to the fort on the Sacramento.

All these people — Jedediah Smith, Joseph Walker, Frémont, the California-bound emigrants — were unwittingly trying to carry out Jefferson's plan for a road west in as straight a line as possible. Although in the East the early trails ran through forests infested with wild animals and Indians, still, there had been trails of sorts. In the Far West no such trails existed. And added to the menace of Indians and wild animals was the constant threat of death from thirst, starvation and cold. In spite of this, these early travelers did find a way from the Great Salt Lake almost due west to the Pacific coast.

The Mormons, who went west the year after the Donner-Reed party, did not follow any part of the National Road. They started from their city, Nauvoo, north of the Road in Illinois. They followed the Oregon Trail to Fort Bridger, then turned southwest through the Wasatch Mountains to reach the lake.

Then, in 1849 came the great Gold Rush to California. Eager to reach the bonanza before all the precious metal was gobbled up by others, the thousands of Forty-Niners took every possible route to their goal. Some embarked at Boston or New York and sailed down around Cape Horn at the tip of South America, then up the Pacific coast to San Francisco. This trip cost $300 and took six months, but they went, singing:

Sutters Office
San Francisco U. C.
August 29th 1848.

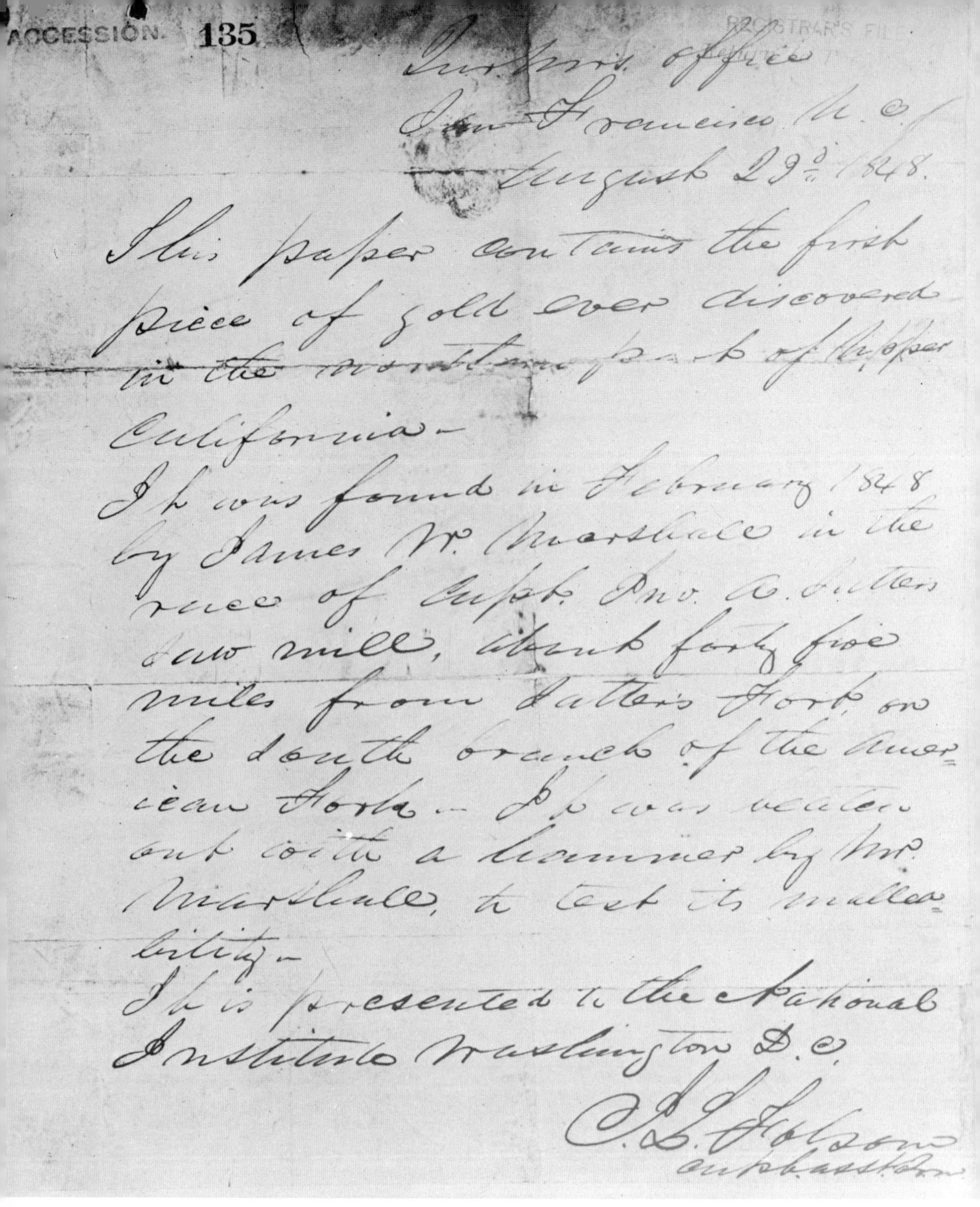

This paper contains the first piece of gold ever discovered in the ~~northern~~ part of Upper California.—

It was found in February 1848 by James W. Marshall in the race of Capt. Ino. A. Sutters saw mill, about forty five miles from Sutter's Fort, on the south branch of the American Fork.— It was beaten out with a hammer by Mr. Marshall, to test its malleability.—

It is presented to the National Institute Washington D. C.

C. L. Folson
ambassador

Centennial Press Service

This letter, in which was wrapped the first gold nugget found in California, was sent to the National Institute in Washington, D.C., in August, 1848.

You get aboard a leaky boat
And sail for San Francisco;
You've got to pump to keep afloat,
Or you don't float, by jingo!
The engine soon begins to squeak,
And not a thing to oil 'er;
Impossible to stop the leak —
Then rip! goes the boiler!

Others left the ship at the mouth of the Chagres River on the Caribbean coast and cut across the Isthmus of Panama to the Pacific. There they took a steamer up to San Francisco. Probably forty thousand people went to California by these two routes.

Many more, who did not want to spend six months on the way or who didn't have the $300, went scurrying overland. They got to Westport Landing (where Kansas City, Missouri, now stands) or St. Joseph, Missouri, any way they could. Many followed the National Road to St. Louis, then up the Missouri to whichever of the two "jumping-off" places they had chosen. At Westport Landing, some turned southwest along the old Santa Fe Trail, then across the southern desert to Los Angeles and north to the "diggings."

Others went on up the river to St. Joseph, then north by land to hit the Oregon Trail on the Platte River. They followed this established route to Fort Bridger, Wyoming. There they turned south to pass through Salt Lake City. This town was less than two years old, but it was a thriving community where the gold-seekers could obtain food and fodder. From this point the Forty-Niners went almost due west to the Humboldt, followed this river for some forty miles, then over the Sierras on the Donner route and down to the Sacramento.

This lucky miner finds "color" in his pan. The little patch of gold is worth from $15 to $20.

State Historical Society of Missouri

Westport Landing, Missouri (where Kansas City now stands) was a busy place during the Gold Rush days, and even earlier. Here emigrants left the boats on which they had come up the Missouri and organized wagon trains for the journey to the Far West.

The Humboldt was an ugly, alkaline stream which the travelers had to use, but hated. Mark Twain said he tried to drink the water but it was like "drinking lye, and not weak lye, either." An Iowa emigrant wrote:

> Meanest and muddiest, filthiest stream,
>   most cordially I hate you.
> What mean these graves so fresh and new
>   along your banks on either side?
> They've all been dug and filled by you,
>   thou guilty wretch! Thou homicide!

113

This cartoon pokes fun at some of the ways suggested for getting to the gold mines of California in the shortest time.

Difficult and unpleasant as this road was, it was heavily traveled in 1849 and 1850. It was known as the California Trail. And though many were dust-sick and starving, some of the folks found the courage to sing as they went. Perhaps it was the jingle:

> Whistle and sing!
> Whistle and sing!
> Shorten the road
> With a laugh as you sing!

Many of the songs of the Gold Rush days are still popular. One of the best known is "Sweet Betsy from Pike":

To the Pacific

Oh, don't you remember sweet Betsy from Pike
Who crossed the wide mountains with her lover Ike;
With two yoke of oxen, a big yellow dog,
A red Shanghai rooster, and one spotted hog.

Another favorite was:

Oh, Susannah!
Oh, don't you cry for me!
I come from Alabama
With my banjo on my knee!

This sketch shows a street in Salt Lake City about the time the Forty-Niners came through it.

STREET IN GREAT SALT LAKE CITY — LOOKING EAST

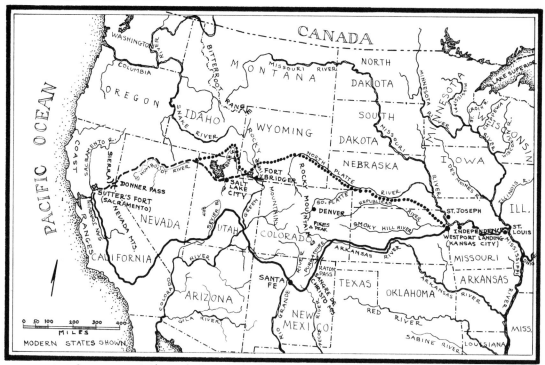

- - - - California Trail through Salt Lake City •••••••• Northern Route to the Gold Fields
——— Southern Route to the Gold Fields

Or:

When I left Missouri River
With my California rig,
I had a shovel, pick and pan,
The things you need to dig.

Thus, during the great Gold Rush the California Trail became so worn with wagon wheels and horses' hooves that traces of it may still be seen in Nevada. And in the museums of the West are ox yokes, whitened wagon wheels, buffalo skulls and other mementos of this busy route across the desert.

10

PIKE'S PEAK OR BUST!

Take up the oxen, boys, and harness up the mules,
Pack away provisions and bring along the tools,
The pick and the shovel and a pan that won't leak,
And we'll start for the gold mines. Hurrah for the Peak!

We'll cross the bold Missouri and we'll steer for the West,
And we'll take the road we think is the shortest and the best.
We'll travel o'er the Plains, where the wind is blowing bleak,
And the sandy washes shall echo with "Hurrah for the Peak!"

This was the song of the gold-seekers of 1859. This was the
voice of the frontier, of the folks in Ohio, Indiana, Illinois and Missouri. The people were all agog. The newspapers were filled with
wild stories. Hundreds were on the move. Those who, ten years
earlier, had been too young or had thought California too far and

the Rockies too dangerous, now could answer the call of gold. Now the Rockies need not be crossed. Now the gold was close by — just across Kansas Territory! And there was more of it, everyone said, than there had been in California.

In August of 1858 a trader from the South Platte River came into Kansas City with a small sack of gold dust. The Kansas City *Journal* announced the great news:

THE NEW ELDORADO! GOLD IN KANSAS TERRITORY!
THE PIKE'S PEAK MINES!!
FIRST ARRIVAL OF GOLD IN KANSAS CITY!!!

Papers all over the country took up the story, each one making the report bigger and better. One told about a small boy who had dug up a thousand dollars worth of gold and who boasted, "I can get all I want without half trying!" Another article said a youth had been found emptying grain sacks, which, he said, he was taking to the diggings to fill them with gold.

An Iowa newspaper described how the gold mining was done:

The gold lies in bands or strata down the slope. The custom of the best miners is to construct heavy wooden sleds with iron ribs, similar to a stone boat. These are taken to the top of the peak, several men get onto each one and guide it down over the strata. The gold curls up on the boat like shavings, and is gathered in as they progress. This is the usual method of collecting it.

No wonder the people were excited. Folks greeted each other

not with "How are you?" but with "What's the news from the dig-gings?"

Stories like the one in the Iowa paper showed that the people knew little about the geography of the region they were writing about. The gold was not on Pike's Peak, at all. The first reported finds were on Cherry Creek, where it now runs through Denver, Colorado. The amount of "color" they "raised" was small, but it was enough to start the wild tales. The peak they talked about was more than seventy miles south of the site.

Perhaps it was natural for folks to think that gold had been found on the famous mountain. Rumors of deposits of the precious metal on the slopes of Pike's Peak had been floating around ever since James Pursley thrilled the Mexicans of Santa Fe with his yarns.

Even before that, travelers into the Southwest had heard legends of gold in that region. There were tales of Indians' using golden bullets in their newly acquired guns, and of Indian chieftains decked with golden ornaments. So it is not surprising that easterners be-lieved the gold lay thick on the mountain slopes. At any rate, Pike's Peak would serve as a guide for their westering wagons.

So the eager gold-seekers tossed their tools and blankets into covered wagons on which they happily painted their famous slogan, "Pike's Peak or Bust!" Or they packed a mule with the bare necessi-ties. Many just tied a frying pan and a coffee pot into their blankets and set out on foot, with their pack on their back. A few, in their haste, tried the new "wind wagons." These were clumsy vehicles to which great canvas sails had been attached in the hope that the wind would waft them swiftly over the prairies. By the spring of 1859 the roads west were crowded.

Poorly equipped and unacquainted with the dangers of the prairie, many a frontiersman set out for the goldfield of western Kansas Territory in high hopes, only to
perish along the way.

By now the steamships were carrying passengers up the Missouri
to Kansas City or Leavenworth, Kansas. These were the "jumping-
off" places for the Fifty-Niners. In these towns the stores were loaded
with blankets, spades, picks and flat iron pans used in getting the
"dust" from the silt of streams. Advertisements warned folks to get
their supplies here, for there were none farther on. The prices were
extremely high, and many a prospector spent his last money here,
unaware that stores already had been set up in the booming settlement on Cherry Creek.

The victims of this gold fever were generally people who had
no idea of the hardship of travel on the Plains. They were mostly
young men, poor farmers, unsuccessful merchants. They had heard
of the fortunes made in California; had probably often dreamed of

THE NATIONAL ROAD

what they would do if ever the chance came their way. Now it had come. Gold — just across a few prairie miles in Kansas Territory.

The great rush began in March, 1859, before the grass was up to feed horses and mules. Hundreds of animals died of starvation. The men were inexperienced, poorly equipped. They did not know where to look for game or how to obtain food, and they, too, died of hunger. It is not known how many perished on the Plains that spring.

There were three main routes to Cherry Creek. One was the northern route — the Oregon Trail — along the Platte to the mouth of the South Platte, and down this stream to the diggings. Those who followed this trail did not have to use the National Road.

The other two routes went along the National Road to St. Charles or St. Louis, Missouri, then up the Missouri River to Kansas City or Leavenworth, Kansas, or to Independence or St. Joseph, Missouri. There the ways parted. One went southwest, along the Santa Fe Trail to Pueblo in what is now Colorado, then north to the goldfield.

The third course was the most popular, because it was the shortest. It was also the most dangerous because it struck out due west across those trackless prairies. This was called the Smoky Hill Trail because it started at the Smoky Hill River, near Fort Riley, Kansas. It lay between the other two roads leading to the new little settlement of Denver.

The dangers on the Smoky Hill Trail were many. There was such a scarcity of food and water that many men and animals perished. Before long the route was known as the Starvation Trail. There were immense distances between stopping places. There was always the threat of Indian attack. Fort Riley, Kansas, had been established

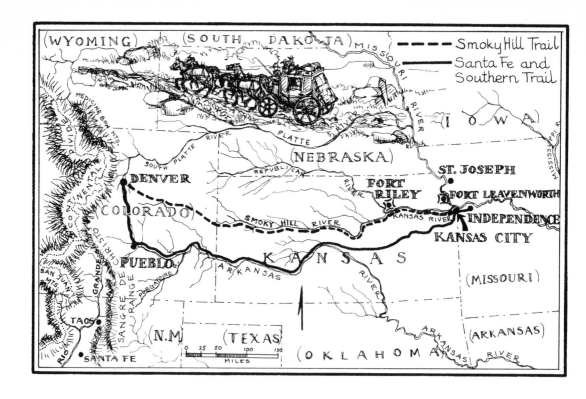

seven years before to protect emigrant trains. But the mounted Indians of the Plains — the Arapaho, Comanche and Cheyenne — were still making raids against the white invaders of their lands.

Hurry as the gold-seekers might, they were doomed to disappointment. The strike on Cherry Creek had not been worth much. Long before the eager throngs reached their goal they learned they had been fooled. The first discoverers of the precious metal had been

This sketch shows the city of Denver, Colorado, in 1859 at the height of the rush to the gold diggings on Cherry Creek.

too optimistic. Exaggerated stories flew eastward to thrill the credulous and set them agog with the hope of easy riches.

The rival discoverers had set up two competing camps, which they later combined to make the town of Denver. Clustered here were the huts and tents of prospectors, shanty saloons and dance halls and other "attractions." But it was certainly not the El Dorado, the Golden City, of the Fifty-Niners' dreams.

Long before the majority could reach Cherry Creek, its bonanza had played out. Trains hurrying westward met discouraged throngs trailing sadly back home. Disappointed, hungry, weary wagoners turned back. They rubbed out the brave slogans and painted, instead, "Pike's Peak and Busted!" Before the summer was over, the tide of travel had turned. There was little singing on the way as hundreds moved sullenly back to their old, everyday jobs, their golden dreams shattered.

Some did not give up so easily. They went on to Denver, lived as best they could, and were on hand when a really great strike was made. The real bonanza was discovered in Clear Creek Canyon in the central Rockies.

When so many people were rushing to the goldfield in western Kansas Territory, the time seemed ripe for starting a commercial stage line. Not long after the first Conestogas dug their wheels into the sandy loam of the prairies to mark out the Smoky Hill Trail, the Butterfield Line sent its stages over this route. The actual name of the line was the Butterfield Overland Dispatch, generally called the B.O.D. It was owned by John Butterfield, one of the great names in overland coaching to the West. A few years later, the Wells Fargo

Company took over the B.O.D. The famous coaches sped over the rutted plains to carry people, supplies and mail to the Rockies, and to fetch back sacks of gold dust to the banks in eastern cities.

Along the stage line, stations were placed ten to twenty-five miles apart, according to the difficulty of the road. The trip from Smoky Hill River to Cherry Creek took from ten to twelve days and cost from $75 to $100. On short runs between stations the charge was twenty-five cents a mile. As many as a hundred Concord stages and a thousand mules were used.

The Concord stagecoach was the last word in western travel. The coaches were built by the Abbott and Downing Company of Concord, New Hampshire; hence their name. The first ones were made before 1830; by 1859 they had been improved and were the usual vehicles for long pulls across rugged land. Drawn by six horses, they made the fastest time possible. But they were not very comfortable. It is told that Horace Greeley, the New York journalist, demanded that the coach in which he was traveling keep a certain schedule. It did. But Mr. Greeley arrived at his destination so shaken up that he was unable to appear and make his speech.

In 1861 Colorado Territory was established from the western section of Kansas Territory. The eastern part became the state of Kansas. For some reason, the very name "Colorado" seemed to have a romantic attraction. Interest in the new territory was high in eastern cities. Many authors and journalists made the difficult trip to the mountains in order to report on the exciting life of the mining camps in the Rockies.

In June of 1866, Bayard Taylor, a famous writer, made the journey over the Smoky Hill Trail to Denver. By this time a traveler could go by train as far as Topeka, Kansas, which Mr. Taylor did. At Topeka he took the stage for Denver. He described his journey in *Colorado: A Summer Trip,* which was avidly read by easterners.

For the most part, Mr. Taylor was pleased with the journey. He praised stagecoach travel, western scenery and mountain air. But he found some inconveniences. The food served at the stopping places was not very palatable, being chiefly pork fat and half-baked biscuits. Accommodations for travelers were the scantiest. At Cheyenne Wells, in Colorado, for example, there was a large stable and plenty of fodder for the mules, but no house at which travelers could rest. Even the people who ran the station were living in a cave under the bluff that rose above the stable. Mr. Taylor saw plenty of buffalo, antelope, rattlesnakes and jack rabbits. The cunning little prairie dogs in their busy communities attracted him. No Indians bothered the coach. He considered the route very good in spite of its nickname, Starvation Trail.

The Smoky Hill Trail across Kansas and Colorado served well until the railroad made it unpopular for a time. It would revive when the automobile became the common means of transportation.

11

ACROSS THE GREAT DIVIDE

On a cold January day in 1859, a lone mountaineer made a camp fire on a sandbar in a small stream. He was high in the Rocky Mountains, in a canyon some thirty-odd miles west of the diggings on Cherry Creek. This solitary fellow was George Jackson, a cousin of Kit Carson. He had been Indian trader, farmer and scout. Now, he was looking for gold.

Jackson thought it logical to look in the canyon. If there was gold in the creek that emptied into the South Platte River, it must have come from someplace, and that place was probably up near the source of the stream. He had looked at several streams, making his fires wherever there was a sandbar that looked promising. The ground, of course, was frozen hard. The fires were intended to thaw out the sand, so it could be washed in the flat iron pan the prospector carried.

All that day he kept his fire going. Occasionally he would kneel and scrape at the sand with his knife to see if it was sufficiently thawed. By nightfall he had not been able to dig into the ground, so he collected a stack of dry bark and limbs from the overhanging pines, and sat beside his fire, feeding it all night long.

In the morning, Jackson pushed aside the embers. Under them the sand was now warm and free. He dug out a panful. Squatting beside the stream, he broke the ice to get water to cover the dirt in the flat iron dish. He held this in his two hands and gently shook it with a sort of circular motion. Swish! Swoosh! From left to right and back again he moved the pan, never taking his eyes from the glistening sand. Even when he caught sight of the color collecting at the edge, he did not pause. His eyes gleamed, that couldn't be helped, but his hands kept up the rhythmic motion.

The first pan held only "fine color," flourlike gold dust. That was not good enough, though of course he carefully scraped it into a cup. For more than an hour he patiently squatted and worked. And at last there it was — a gleaming nugget the size of the tip of his finger. That was all he needed.

Very carefully, Jackson covered over the hole he had dug in the sandbar. Then he marked a nearby fir tree so he could find this very bar again. Too many reported discoveries had been lost by carelessly placed signs. When he was sure that he could rediscover the exact spot, but that no one else would be able to interpret his markings, he gathered up his belongings and went down to Denver.

Jackson kept his discovery a close secret until spring. Then he returned to the canyon, found his sandbar, and set to work. In a short time he had panned several thousand dollars worth of gold. Now his find could no longer be kept secret. The news spread like

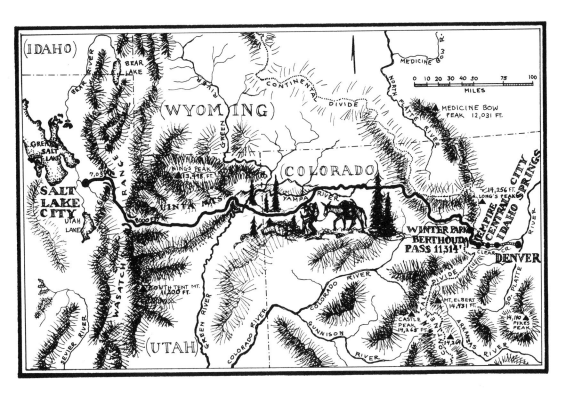

prairie fire, and the rush to the Clear Creek area was on. This was the real bonanza.

The canyon became a hodge-podge of tents, shanties and dug-outs. All sorts of mining machinery was used, from the simple iron pan to elaborate, crazily constructed mechanisms for separating the precious metal from the sand and rock. Some, who thought the pan was too slow, hollowed out a log and filled the cavity with the pay

All sorts of homemade machinery were used at the Clear Creek diggings. Here a miner sifts gold-bearing rocks and dirt on a rickety screen he himself constructed. The bucket at the top of the slide dumps the material over the screen, through which the finer dirt falls.

dirt and water. This was rocked back and forth to cause the separation. This sort of contrivance was called the Long Tom.

Now there had to be a road of some sort, over which the men could get to the mines, and over which the gold could be taken away. It did not take long to construct such a road from Denver to Clear Creek, along which sprang up some of the West's most famous mining towns: Idaho Springs, Dumont, Empire, where the road ended. It looked as if it could never go farther with the snowy peaks of the Continental Divide barring its way.

The Continental Divide is just that. It is the high backbone of the continent. From its eastern slopes all streams empty into the Gulf of Mexico or the Atlantic Ocean. Waters to the west of the crest flow to the Gulf of California or the Pacific. Getting over this thousands-

Prospectors and emigrants lost many animals when they tried to cross the Rockies in winter to reach the mining camps.

Library of Congress

PROSPECTORS AND EMIGRANTS CROSSING THE PARKS AMONG THE MOUNTAINS, 10,000 FEET ABOVE THE SEA, EN ROUTE TO LEADVILLE — LOSS OF ANIMALS ON THE ROAD.

of-feet-high, rocky ridge had long been difficult for westering emigrants. In 1824 Jedediah Smith had discovered a gentle incline in what is now Wyoming, and which became known as the South Pass. Over it went the first wagons to the Far West. John C. Frémont had explored several passes through the Rockies and over the Divide. Now the men began to look for a way west out of Clear Creek Canyon.

There was good reason for wanting to go due west from the mines. On the other side of the mountains lay Utah, with Salt Lake City at this time larger than Denver. Farther on lay San Francisco, its harbor always filled with ships. It seemed that it would be cheaper to take the gold westward across one fourth of the nation, after which it could travel cheaply by sea, than to transport it east over three times as many miles.

Emigrants coming to the Great Salt Lake Valley from the East would get their first view of the valley with the Great Salt Lake beyond.

San Francisco Harbor was always filled with ships, which could carry the gold from Colorado more cheaply than it could be transported eastward by land.

So, about the time Colorado became a territory, E. L. Berthoud of Denver set out to survey a road due west from Empire, the last settlement in Clear Creek Canyon. He was accompanied by Jim Bridger, famous mountain man, scout and Indian trader. Bridger had been in the mountains and beyond for forty years. He knew the country as few others ever did.

The two men, with a small party, started from Empire, moving up the canyon. Before they had gone ten miles they were stopped by a seemingly impossible ridge. Bridger went one way, Berthoud the other, looking for some place where they could get over this barrier. Berthoud was the lucky searcher. He spied where the north fork of Clear Creek tumbled out of the heights. He clambered along the stream bed till he could go no farther; then he turned from the creek and made his way right up the mountainside. At the top he found a small stream flowing northwest instead of eastward. He was

133

Jim Bridger, famous mountain man, guide, and Indian trader, who was with Edward L. Berthoud when that explorer discovered Berthoud Pass over the Rocky Mountains.

Empire, the last town in Clear Creek Canyon, from which Berthoud's party set out to find a route over the mountains.

on the Divide! Ahead lay a parklike bowl, grassy and flower-strewn, such as occur here and there high in the Rockies.

Berthoud searched along the Divide for its lowest hollow, which turned out to be more than eleven thousand feet above sea level. But it offered a pass of sorts. A road could be built here. When Bridger found him, the old scout agreed this was the best way for the road to go. The party returned to Denver and to an enthusiastic welcome. They were commissioned to explore the route on, over the pass, across the western slopes and on to Salt Lake City.

135

Edward L. Berthoud

Edward L. Berthoud, who discovered Berthoud Pass over the Rockies west of Denver.

This photograph shows the western slope of Berthoud Pass in Colorado. In the distance are impassable heights.

They left Denver in July of 1861. Some thirty miles beyond the pass, they reached a river flowing westward, and decided that this must be the headwaters of rivers Bridger had known in Utah so many years ago when he was trapping beaver in that region.

The route they followed was difficult, but very beautiful. The slopes were heavily timbered; the ground bright with wild flowers — the delicate blue and cream columbine; the wild yellow pea, wild

This is the view of the Great Salt Lake which Berthoud and his party would have seen as they came out of the mountains east of the Great Salt Lake Valley.

roses and the lovely mariposa lilies. Sparkling streams meandered through the grass. Deer and elk roamed unafraid. This had once been a favorite hunting ground of the Utes and small bands of the natives still haunted the groves.

Berthoud's party came to the Yampa River and followed it for awhile. When it joined the southward-flowing Green, the men left it and made their way west and north to the city that was their goal.

Their report convinced officials that a road could be constructed almost due west from Denver to Salt Lake City. Parties were sent out to survey and plan. However, not much was actually done. Few travelers attempted this route which was so beautiful, but buried beneath deep snows in winter and flooded by swollen streams in spring.

It was not until thirteen years after Berthoud's discovery of the pass named for him that a wagon road was built here. By this time the railroad stretched clear across the nation, and a wagon road over the Rockies was not much needed. In fact, this beautiful route has never been the most popular way between Denver and Salt Lake City.

Even within Colorado it was not much used. Ute hunting parties unwittingly followed it at times and raiding bands must have galloped along it. One of the conflicts between American soldiers and Indians took place within a few miles of the road. In September 1879, Nathan C. Meeker, agent at the White River Indian reservation, feared an uprising. He sent out a call for troops. The soldiers came down from Rawlins, Wyoming. When they insisted on entering the reservation, which the government had pledged no troops would be permitted to do, the angry Utes ambushed and killed or wounded more than half of the soldiers in the invading party.

For years, this section of the road west was the least finished

The clear-cut, imposing beauty of the high Rockies is evident in this photograph of the Mosquito Range in central Colorado. This range boasts some of the highest peaks in the state.

and used of all the highway from the Atlantic to the Pacific. In 1910, Utah took a hand and put its segment under the state road commission. Nine years later it became a part of the Victory Highway. This was another attempt to build a "due west" road across the entire country. To carry out the patriotic national idea, the markers along this road were red, white and blue.

However, none of this segment of road was ever made into a truly modern road until the automobile became common. Then the extraordinary scenery and the long stretches of unspoiled, unoccupied country began to attract those who wanted to get away from the hustle and bustle of the city.

12

THE GREAT ROAD TODAY

Sunday, July 3, 1938, was a great day in Colorado. Crowds thronged the streets of Denver. Governors, Senators, mayors and prominent businessmen, the lovely "queens" of various state celebrations, and many an old-timer made their way up a newly paved road to Berthoud Pass, where a rope across the highway was cut by Governor Teller Ammons of Colorado. Governor Henry Blood of Utah made a speech. Flags waved in the mountain air; bands played patriotic tunes.

It was just such a celebration as had been held at St. Clairsville, Ohio, a hundred and thirteen years before. Only this time the rejoicing was over the completion, not the beginning, of a great road. U.S. 40, from New Jersey to California, was now a modern, wide and hard-surfaced highway. It had taken nearly three hundred years to grow from the "street that leads to ye woods."

The roads by which wagons, mule trains and stagecoaches trav-

Some of the celebrants at the opening of Berthoud's Pass and the completion of the coast-to-coast highway in Colorado on July 3, 1938.

eled had served the country well until the transcontinental railroad made such highways unnecessary for long-distance journeys. On May 10, 1869, the Union Pacific and the Central Pacific railroads met at Promontory, Utah. That meeting meant the end of most stagecoach and mule train travel.

The great years of the railroad have been called the Dark Age of the highways. It did not last long. Within thirty years of the union of the rails at Promontory, American "horseless carriages" or "buggynauts" were being constructed. By 1914, Henry Ford was using the assembly line method in manufacturing automobiles. This new procedure made cars much cheaper and more numerous.

At the same time, Americans were growing wealthier, were demanding better living conditions, and were buying the tools and implements, the machines and appliances to help them realize their ambitions for an easier life. The idea of the automobile struck the popular fancy. Folks began to buy cars and to use them. They started driving over the old, bumpy dirt or gravel roads that had served for wagon travel, but were very hard on the new machines. New and better highways were needed.

At first local governments tried to meet this need, just as they had at first built the roads for the stagecoaches. This resulted in a very uneven development: some states would have good roads while their neighbors might have only very primitive ones. It was soon plain that, as with the National Road, the cause of cross-country highways was one that needed Federal help.

By 1912 a group of far-seeing businessmen (chiefly connected with the automobile industry) saw that something definite must be done. They formed an association to promote a transcontinental highway. To indicate their patriotic motive they chose the name Lincoln Highway Association, and the colors red, white and blue for their signs and markers. They planned to see that a coast-to-coast highway was constructed.

Things worked out about as they had more than a hundred years earlier when the National Road was planned. Cities began demanding that the great highway pass through them. Of course this was impossible. Such a road could not jog hither and thither so as to accommodate every town that wanted to be included.

So other "transcontinental" roads were laid out, though they did not even aim at crossing the entire country. It just made people happier to be able to say they were on a "transcontinental highway," whether that was really so or not. By the 1920's there were more than two hundred such roads. Each had chosen a different color to mark its route. Often the telegraph poles along the way were used as signposts. Sometimes these poles were merely painted the color chosen for the highway. If several roads went over the same route for some distance, the poles with their Easter-egg colors were very confusing to the motorist. There was no government supervision, and anyone who wanted to could mark his own "highway." Even if a state tried to control the situation, its efforts only added to the perplexity.

In 1925 the Bureau of Public Roads (now in the Department of Commerce) was in the Department of Agriculture. The problem of highways had become so pressing that the Secretary of Agriculture named a board to study it. Now the Federal Government was taking a hand, just as it had done back in 1806.

The board studied the mishmash of roads across the country

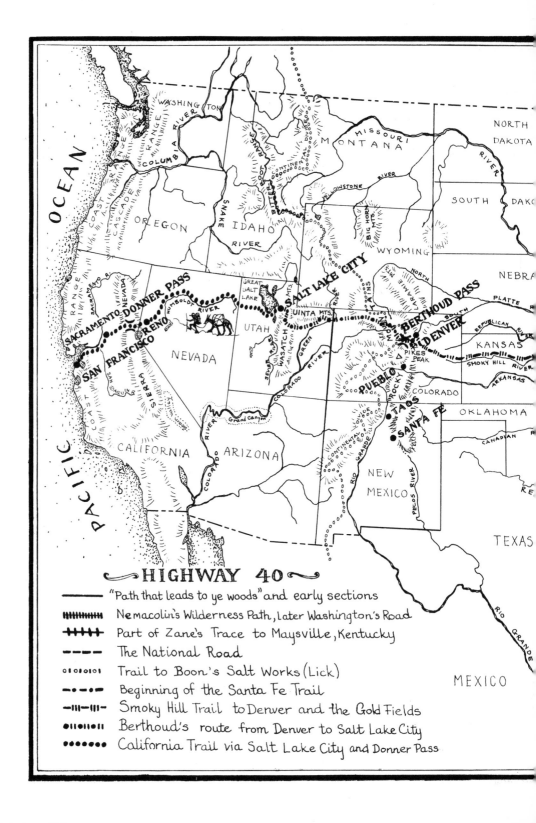

⌒HIGHWAY 40⌒

———	"Path that leads to ye woods" and early sections
╫╫╫╫╫╫	Nemacolin's Wilderness Path, Later Washington's Road
┿┿┿┿┿	Part of Zane's Trace to Maysville, Kentucky
– – – –	The National Road
01010101	Trail to Boon's Salt Works (Lick)
–·–·–·	Beginning of the Santa Fe Trail
–III–III–	Smoky Hill Trail to Denver and the Gold Fields
•II•II•II	Berthoud's route from Denver to Salt Lake City
••••••••	California Trail via Salt Lake City and Donner Pass

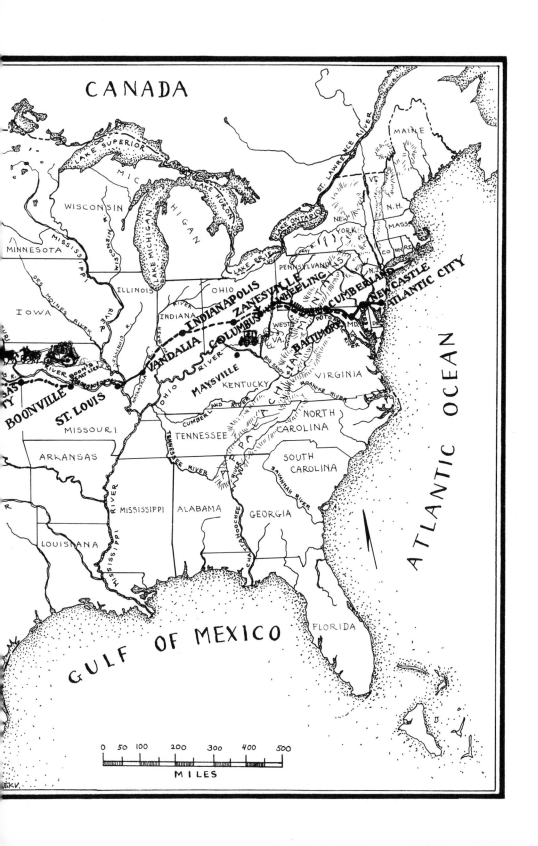

In 1949 many Western towns re-created the rush to the goldfields that had taken place 100 years earlier. This picture shows a part of the equipment used in Las Vegas, Nevada, in the observance of the Gold Rush Centennial.

and decided to lay out a system of highways, each one having an important and definite route. Each would be numbered, rather than named. Those running east and west would be given even numbers such as 10, 30, 40. Those running north and south would have odd numbers ending in digits such as 1, 5 or 9. This scheme proved so popular that states adopted it and began to number their roads. Today such terms as "U.S. 40" or "State 36" are a part of our daily conversation.

148

U.S. 40 was born at this time, in the mid-1920's. It was decided in this case that a coast-to-coast route had already been marked out by westering travel. It would be rather easy to follow the old paths, trails and traces. And it was desirable to have one highway across the central portion of the country. There would be other roads to the north and the south, but the most central section should have its own transcontinental route. This was U.S. 40 and this is where the original National Road played its part. For U.S. 40 follows this road for many miles through the Midwest. Even more important, perhaps, is the fact that the bill passed by Congress in 1806, authorizing the construction of the National Road, had made it possible for the Federal Government to aid in the construction of this great modern highway.

Traces of the original road may be seen in some places, lying close beside the paved ribbon of U.S. 40. In other areas, these vestiges lie a few miles to one side, or have been covered over by a side road or an alternate route. An extra segment has been added at the eastern extremity, from New Castle, Delaware, to Atlantic City, New Jersey, so the highway truly goes from coast to coast. The entire route meets President Jefferson's hope of a road "due west to bind the nation together."

Since the road grew from east to west, let us follow Highway 40 from the Atlantic to the Pacific. It will be a sketchy journey. We shall first make note only of the states and capitals through which it passes.

Starting at Atlantic City, New Jersey, U.S. 40 crosses the southern portion of that state to New Castle, Delaware. Only the northern tip of that tiny state is traversed; then into Maryland, across its northern section, the southwest corner of Pennsylvania, and the northern tip of West Virginia. Now the highway crosses the central part of Ohio and Indiana, and slants down through Illinois. It passes through the capitals of the first two of this trio of midwestern states, but misses Springfield, the capital of Illinois. You will remember, however, that when the National Road was built, it did go through Vandalia, which was then the Illinois capital. Highway 40 cuts across the approximate center of Missouri and Kansas, somewhat north of the center of Colorado, Utah and Nevada, and runs into and across California to the Pacific at San Francisco. It goes through the capitals of all these western states save Missouri and Nevada, but these two interesting cities lie only a few miles south of the highway. A traveler over this route thus sees part of fourteen states and visits six state capitals.

While he is thinking about capitals, he will recall that from Baltimore it is only thirty-six miles south to the national capital at Washington, D. C.

If the traveler is interested in eras, in historical values, he will find much to please him. In Utah, he may travel just seven miles north of the highway at Jensen to the Dinosaur National Monument to view the graveyard of these great prehistoric monsters. Or he may study a later period, when Indians were the only inhabitants of this land, in several places. Six miles north of Hebron, Ohio, are great Indian mounds, built by the prehistoric people of this region. In the West the highway passes through land rich in Indian lore; Apache, Comanche, Arapaho, Ute, Paiute and various small tribes of California dwelt in this central region of the country. Trappers, explorers and soldiers found these tribes in a far different situation

THE COURSE OF EMPIRE.

This illustration from *Harper's*, June, 1866, shows an emigrant train entering an Indian village. The warriors in the foreground look desperate enough to frighten the travelers.

from that they enjoy today. The museums in the various cities of this area have much to enrich one's understanding of these early inhabitants.

The highway carries one past many relics of the early white settlers. There is the Old Church built in 1704 at New Castle, Delaware; the Friends' (Quakers) meeting house in Baltimore; the oldest log house west of the Mississippi at Fort Zumwalt in Mis-

At several places along the old National Road are monuments such as this: the Madonna of the Trail, honoring the emigrant women who traveled westward.

souri; or the home of the Boones not far from the road. Directions to most of these early buildings are marked, so that they are easy to find.

Also well-marked are sites of interest in the French and Indian War, the Revolution, the War of 1812, and the Civil War. It is worth the time and effort to stop a moment to view these places; to let your eyes see what our heroes once saw; to let your feet tread the ground they made historic. Only a few such sites need be mentioned: Fort Necessity, Braddock's grave, Fort McHenry and the town of Frederick, Maryland. It was in this town, so the poet John Greenleaf Whittier writes, that Barbara Frietchie gave Stonewall Jackson a lesson in patriotism. Whether this actually happened or not, one may visit the Barbara Frietchie House in Frederick and see many interesting relics.

All along Highway 40 are reminders of heroic happenings. At Wheeling, West Virginia, one thinks back to the story of Elizabeth Zane and of how she braved Indian arrows to carry ammunition to the beleaguered men in Fort Henry. Passing along Gallatin Street, Vandalia, one recalls Albert Gallatin's long support of the National Road, and Missouri is full of mementos of Daniel Boone and his family. Even the hundreds of unrecorded women are honored along this historic route. At several places such as Vandalia are Madonna of the Trail monuments, showing an emigrant mother with her children, her face to the West.

Toll houses, old taverns and bridges speak of the days when this was the great channel of travel east and west. At Cumberland, Maryland are many such mementos: a log house believed to have been used by Washington; a monument to Thomas Cresap, and many others.

In the late 1860's, camels carried salt from Wells to Virginia City, Nevada, where it was used in treating silver ores.

Of special interest are some of the bridges: the famous *Y* bridge at Zanesville; the old *S* bridge near New Concord, Ohio. The iron bridge at Brownsville, Pennsylvania was built across the Monongahela as the result of an accident. Once when Henry Clay was traveling the great Road, the coach tipped over, dumping the statesman into the mud. He got up, shook himself and declared, "Clay and mud will never again be mixed on this spot!" And when he reached Washington, he set to work to have this strong bridge erected over the stream.

Besides all this history there are a multitude of wonderful things to be seen: the boardwalk at Atlantic City; the rows of red brick

At the western end of U.S. 40 stands the Golden Gate Bridge arching over the mouth of San Francisco Bay.

houses with white marble steps in Baltimore; the Monument Circle in Indianapolis with its surrounding "mile square," all planned and laid out by Alexander Ralston, who helped plan Washington, D. C. The Bellefontaine Cemetery in St. Louis with the graves of early

155

The Bonneville Salt Flats in western Utah where many a land-speed record has been set.

settlers, trappers and statesmen. Denver, the "mile high" city, and Salt Lake, the city of the Mormons. There one can see the Kennecott copper mine at Bingham, the largest man-made excavation in the world. Farther west are Utah's Bonneville Salt Flats, where many a world land-speed record has been made. And Wells, Nevada, from which camels in the 1860's carried salt to the silver mines at Virginia City. And, at last, San Francisco with its Golden Gate harbor and bridge and its amusing cable cars.

History and wonders galore make an adventure of almost every mile of the cross-country journey on U.S. 40.

Thus, the National Road lives again in this transcontinental highway — larger than the original, older, more modern, but still the embodiment of the dreams of Washington, Jefferson, Thomas Worthington, Henry Clay and other patriots; still a "road due West to bind the nation together."

INDEX

ABOUT THE AUTHOR

Olive W. Burt is the author of more than forty books. A resident of Salt Lake City, Utah, she is an inveterate traveler in all parts of the world, especially the United States, and a lover of American history.